OVERTHINKING

A Guide for Highly Sensitive People. Stop Overthinking and Build Unbeatable Mental Toughness, Develop Self Discipline, Self Confidence, Love, and Compassion

Krystal Zhurov

Table of Contents

Introduction: What is Overthinking

Are you someone who thinks too much about things? What do you think? According to psychologists, who have conducted extensive research in this area, thinking too much means "thinking too much, unnecessarily, and passively." And constantly think about the meanings, causes, and consequences of your character, feelings, and above all your problems."

Examples of thinking too much include asking yourself over and over during the day why you suddenly feel so old or if your mild headache could be a symptom of something troubling and maybe even potential death. It might mean staying up at night thinking, "This economy is so bad that my investments won't be worth it; I'll definitely lose my job and never be able to send my kids to college." Or it could mean thinking many times throughout the day about the lack of attraction of your thin and weak hair. Thinking too much is precisely what it equates to, thinking too much. When you think too much, in place of acting and doing things, you think too much. When you analyze, review, and also repeat the same thoughts over and over, instead of acting, you think too much.

This habit prevents you from acting. Spend energy, disable your ability to make decisions, and put you in the circle of thinking over and over again.

It is the kind of thought that was his time and energy that prevented him from acting, doing new things, and moving forward in his life. Words like tying a rope that is connected to a pole and circling over and over. In this situation, there is a greater risk of worry, anxiety, and lack of inner peace. On the other hand, when you think too much, you become more efficient, calmer, and happier.

Too much thinking is as debilitating as usual. This can prevent you from enjoying social events, interfere with sleep, affect your work performance, and even ruin your vacation. As a general rule, chronic over-thinking also accompanies all physical anxiety. This means that too much thinking leaves you not only mentally disturbed but also exhausted. If you know that picture, you're probably desperate for a way to stop thinking about your life too much and start living. However, you may have tried to change that and considered it an insurmountable obstacle.

It is imperative to know that it is possible to learn to overcome excessive thinking. Whether you understand how to stop thinking too much about a relationship, how to stop thinking obsessively about your health, or how to enjoy socialization without panic, there are powerful techniques you can learn.

What Happens During You Overthink?

- Just stop thinking about an event, person, something that happened in the past, or a problem. Instead of looking for a solution, take the initiative and be active; just think and get it out of your mind. Sometimes, when something bad happens, you think about worst-case scenarios, with thoughts like "what if?" Or "why?"
- Occasionally switch to negative thinking patterns.
- You are worried about past mistakes or current problems and issues and how they may lead to negative results.
- You are obsessed or over-analyzing your daily experiences and your interactions with people.
- You inflate every word, every thought, and every event beyond the real and reasonable scale, reading the things that really exist there.

If this happens often, you call psychologists a ruminant or an over-thinker.

Chapter 1:
Is Overthinking Bad?

Overthinking is an issue since it really meddles with sensible decision making. Try not to confound "sensible speculation" with overthinking. Software engineers, for instance, must foresee a client's needs in whatever number zones as could be allowed to protect a quality item. That isn't overthinking. That is their activity. Yet, If a software engineer continually audits what has been created regardless of consolations, all is alright, chases for blunders again and again, or keeps awake until late engrossed, at that point, the individual is overthinking. Overthinkers waste energy. The passionate expense or time-cost is excessively high, and the advantage is excessively low. Overthinkers waver—they are excessively mindful—and frequently pass up on chances or avoid making any genuine move. Overthinkers don't think about that more often than not in life. We need to respond to occasions as they happen in light of the fact that they are unexpected. Regardless of how well we plan, there is continually something that doesn't go as arranged—there are delays, things break, people meddle, the climate meddles, we become sick - SOMETHING happens that we should fight with.

What's more, learn to expect the unexpected. WE COME OUT JUST FINE ALMOST ALL THE TIME. At the end of the day, overthinking can't set us up that well for the unexpected, and regardless of whether the unexpected occurs, the vast majority handle it alright more often than not. Overthinking can cause examination loss of motion whereby no move is made — or it isn't taken in a timely way.

Overthinkers regularly bother people around them. Actually, others may make up for your overthinking by getting excessively easygoing, excessively impulsive, and also "accept circumstances for what they are"— which can add to your pressure. Overthinkers make decision exhaustion. That is a procedure whereby a lot of fixating and investigation makes mental exhaustion with the goal that decisions made later in the day or week become impulsive or foolish—the polar opposite of overthinking. A straightforward model would be somebody who can't decide what to order at a café — they read and re-read — they attempt to settle on what is sound "Discovering Peace When Your Heart Is in Pieces" "Discovering Peace When Your Heart Is in Pieces" and what isn't, what is excessively expensive, if should they be brave and order something new or order something they've had previously, or should they think about what others may think about their decision. They just over-break down, and when the server asks them what they need, they state, "Gracious, hell, I couldn't care less. I'll have the extraordinary." at the end of the day, people who overthink things they can't do much about become exhausted and don't generally settle on sensible decisions about things they CAN take care of on the grounds that they are simply too darn tired of reasoning!

Maybe they told you something was wrong because you feel anxiety and tension when dealing with strong and aggressive people or when exposed to constant stimuli throughout the day.

"I want these neighbors to reject their music. I still endure it like crazy."

"What music? I hear one. You should let the noise bother you. There's something wrong with you."

"You're so touched," "Who cares?", "Why can't you let it go?" "Stop being so sensitive," "You're too isolated." "Why do you always overdo it?" "You're the cause you don't have any friends."

Chapter 2:
Symptoms And Signs Of Overthinking

It's valuable to have a complete list of overthinking disorder side effects. This enables you to distinguish when you are truly getting into a perilous area for your emotional well-being.

Taking a gander at the accompanying manifestations can assist you with leading an overthinking disorder test.

You can't rest.

At the point when you attempt, you can't turn off your psyche, and you start to feel fomented by stresses or questions.

You self-sedate.

Concentrates on overthinking disorder recommend you may turn to drugs, liquor, nourishment, or other outer methods for directing your feelings. This is on the grounds that you don't feel ready to quiet down utilizing our inside assets.

You're constantly worn out.

This might be from sleep deprivation or just from the steady circle of your disturbed contemplations.

You need to control everything.

You attempt to design each part of your life, down to the last detail. This is the main way you feel safe; however, it never fully works (since it's difficult to control everything).

You fixate on failure.

You will, in general, be a fussbudget and regularly envision how dreadful it is to flop in any capacity. This fear of failure frequently deadens you, keeping you from gaining from any errors.

You fear what's to come.

Rather than being energized by all you've yet to achieve and encounter, you are caught in your very own nervousness about what could turn out badly.

You don't confide in your very own judgment.

You re-think yourself on everything based on what you're wearing to where you're going, what you're stating, and how you go over to other people. Also, you may depend on others to promise you that your judgment is sound.

You get pressure migraines.

These seem like a tight band around your waist, and you may likewise see torment or firmness in your neck. Ceaseless pressure migraines are an indication that you frantically need a rest.

Chapter 3:
How To Stop Overthinking

Overcoming obsessive thoughts requires an activity plan. If you need to stop overthinking, you have to discover direct strategies that work and rehash them until they become natural. You may likewise profit by treatment or therapeutic intercessions if your tension is particularly crippling, yet you can utilize useful activities related to these medicines.

Listed below are five of the most effective ways to defeat overthinking and put a stop to your persistent circle of considerations. As you become acclimated to them, you can adjust and change them to suit you. Along these lines, continue perusing to find how to stop overthinking today!

Ways To Stop Overthinking Now

You, at last, have a couple of calm minutes to yourself, possibly to quickly begin thinking about whether you neglected to send that thank-you email or whether you've overestimated your odds of getting the advancement.

Sound commonplace? Stressing and overthinking are pieces of the human experience; however, when left unchecked, they can negatively affect your prosperity.

All in all, what's an overthinking individual to do? These tips can assist you in moving the correct way.

Know about Your Thought Process

Fanatical overthinking is distinctive for everybody. It develops a more profound degree of familiarity with your overthinking, asking inquiries concerning for what good reason and when it happens.

Start giving nearer consideration to your points of view, and notice when you're thinking in a useless manner. Note down what you're thinking and the structure of it.

For instance, would you say you are replaying a past discussion on a circle, investigating it for your failures?

On the other hand, would you say you are envisioning future calamity situations in your creative mind? What's more, composing what you think actuated the overthinking. Is it okay to say that it was something to do with social cooperation? Vulnerability? Setting off to another condition?

This gives you ammo to challenge the fundamental constraining convictions through reflection or diary work. In time, you will have the option to appropriate triggers before they cause a genuine scene of overthinking, mediating with a portion of the further strategies recorded underneath. In the end, the expectation is that the triggers will likewise turn out to be less amazing in light of the fact that you'll comprehend their inceptions and expertise to retaliate in your brain.

How To Stop Overthinking Using Organization Tips.

One of the most efficient ways to stop overthinking is to outfit new pragmatic ways of managing life's difficulties. Consider the accompanying tips specifically when attempting to figure out how to stop overthinking:

Embrace a more extensive point of view.

When something is pestering you, ask yourself: will this matter in a year? What about a month? What about half a month? Regularly, you'll see it won't matter even a month down the line. This can enable you to unwind.

Settle on time-constrained decisions. For instance, you may give yourself five minutes to decide about something minor (for example, regardless of whether you're setting off to some housework or whether you'll go to the rec center today). In the meantime, you may take all things considered thirty minutes to decide on a greater issue like whether to give an introduction or go to a major get-together.

Take breaks for the duration of the day. It is decreased by large tension levels by taking ordinary breaks to do quieting things (for example, 10 minutes of reflection, 30 minutes of perusing a fiction book, or 20 minutes of strolling in the recreation center).

Limit overpowering information. It's likewise useful to set time restrictions on things like working with messages, perusing online networking, and so on. If one of your triggers is this sort of tactile over-burden, you may give yourself 15 minutes four times per day for these assignments, yet no more. Get Active! Retrain Your Brain To Think Positively

Learning how to stop overthinking, nervousness, and eagerness likewise have a great deal to improve associations with your physical body. Both physical and mental types of positive incitement help to revise tricky, negative manners of thinking. For instance:

Exercise can do something amazing for the over-mastermind. It concentrates the psyche on something clear, organized, and fulfilling, turning repressed energy into something you can utilize. It likewise floods the body with feel-great endorphins that make you progressively positive by and large. Discover something you really love, regardless of whether it's a group activity, running in a delightful spot, cycling with companions, or swimming laps after work.

Connect with your brain in learning something new. Get another dialect, take a stab at something innovative you've never endeavored, make sense of how to play another critical thinking game (for example, chess, Sudoku, or Scrabble), or take up some type of making.

You can rehearse contemplation for overthinking. Straightforward, 10-minute body examining practices function admirably here. Inhale profoundly for a couple of moments. At that point, think about the sensations in each piece of your body, working from head to do. Notice strain, and discharge it. Then again, profound breathing additionally functions admirably alone. Take in through the nose for two seconds and out through the mouth for four. This example is demonstrated to be the most unwinding.

Be Patient And Live In The Present

Learning to stop thinking and worrying also involves cultivating ways to live better in the present moment. First, you should be wary of vague fears about what might happen to you. Instead, face the hardest question: what's the worst that could happen? More than once, it won't be as bad as you think.

In addition, he generally finds that he has the resources to deal with the worst-case scenario. Second, use techniques that anchor you in the present moment. When you think too much, endeavor to slow down physically. Try to take note of every movement of your muscles and everything around you. Your brain will need time to respond. You can also try telling the present in your head (for example, "Now I'm walking. I'm dressing now") to bring it back to the present.

Take a step backward and take note of how you react.

The way you react to your thoughts can sometimes lead you into a cycle of rumination or repetition. Do you feel irritated, nervous, or wrong? What is the main emotion behind your thoughts?

Having self-awareness is the key to changing your thinking.

Discover a distraction

Close down overthinking by including yourself in an action you appreciate.

This appears to be unique for everybody, except thoughts include:

learning some new kitchen abilities by handling another formula

setting off to your preferred exercise class

taking up another leisure activity, for example, painting

volunteering with a nearby association

It tends to be difficult to begin something new when you're overpowered by your thoughts. If finding an interruption feels overwhelming, have a go at putting aside a little lump of time — state, 30 minutes — each other day. Utilize this time to either investigate potential interruptions or fiddle with existing ones.

Take a full breath

You've heard it a million times; however, that is on the grounds that it works. Whenever you end up hurling and turning over your thoughts, close your eyes, and inhale profoundly.

Attempt it

Here's a decent starter exercise to assist you with loosening up with your breath:

Locate an agreeable spot to sit and loosen up your neck and shoulders.

Spot one hand over your heart and the other over your gut.

Inhale and exhale through your nose, focusing on how your chest and stomach move as you relax.

Take a stab at doing this activity three times every day for 5 minutes, or at whatever point you have dashing thoughts.

Reflect

Building up a customary contemplation practice is a proof upheld approach to help clear your brain of anxious babble by turning your consideration internal.

Not certain how to begin? We have everything you have to know in this how-to control. All you require is 5 minutes and a calm spot.

Take a look at the master plan.

In what capacity will every one of the issues skimming around in your mind influence you or in quite a while from now? Will anybody truly mind that you purchased an organic product plate for the potluck as opposed to heating a pie without any preparation?

Don't let minor issues turn into noteworthy obstacles.

Accomplish something pleasant for another person

Attempting to facilitate the heap for another person can assist you with placing things in context. Consider ways you can be of administration to somebody experiencing a troublesome time.

Does your companion who's in a separation need a couple of long stretches of childcare? Would you be able to get staple goods for your neighbor who's been wiped out?

Acknowledging you have the ability to fill somebody's heart with joy better can prevent negative thoughts from taking over. It additionally gives you something gainful to concentrate on rather than your endless stream of thoughts.

Recognize automatic negative thinking

Automated negative thoughts (ANTs) allude to automatic negative thoughts; typically including fear or outrage, you sometimes have in response to a situation.

Handling ANTs

You can find out and work through your ANTs by tracking your thoughts and effectively working to transform them:

Utilize a notebook to follow the situation giving you nervousness, your disposition, and the primary idea that comes to you naturally.

As you delve into subtleties, assess why the situation is causing these negative thoughts.

Separate the feelings you're encountering and attempt to identify what you're informing yourself regarding the situation.

Locate an option in contrast to your unique idea. For instance, rather than bouncing directly to, "This will be an epic failure," have a go at something along the lines of, "I'm truly trying my best."

Recognize your success

At the point when you're amidst overthinking, stop and take out your notebook or your preferred note-taking application on your telephone. Scribble down five things that have gone directly over the previous week and your job in them.

These must be great achievements. Maybe this week you stayed in your coffee budget or cleaned your car. When you look at it on paper or on the screen, you will be surprised how these little things pile up.

If this seems helpful, check this list when you find your thoughts spiraling.

Stay tuned

Not ready to go into a meditation routine? There are many other ways to anchor in the present moment.

Be here now

Here are some ideas:

Disconnect. Turn off your computer or phone for a day every day and devote time to the activity.

Eat carefully. Enjoy one of your favorite dishes. Try to find joy in every bite and really focus on the taste, smell, and sensation of food in your mouth.

Step outside the Walk Out, even if it's just a quick walk around the block. List what you see along the way, observing the smells or sounds you hear.

Think about different perspectives

Sometimes, calming your thoughts requires venturing outside of your standard point of view. How you see the world is molded by your background, qualities, and suppositions. Envisioning things from an alternate perspective can assist you with working through a portion of the commotion.

Jot down a portion of the thoughts swirling around in your head. Attempt to explore how substantial every one is. For instance, perhaps you're worried about a forthcoming excursion since you simply realize it will be a catastrophe. However, is that actually what will occur? What sort of evidence do you need to back that up?

Make a move

Sometimes, you may go over similar thoughts more than once in light of the fact that you aren't taking any solid activities about a specific situation.

Can't stop thinking about somebody you envy? Rather than having it ruin your day, let your feelings assist you with settling on better decisions.

Whenever you're visited by the green-looked at the beast, be proactive and jot down ways you can approach arriving at your objectives. This will move you out of your own head and channel your energy into taking significant advances.

Practice self-compassion

Harping on past missteps prevents you from giving up. In case you're thumping yourself over something you did a week ago, give pulling together a shot of self-compassion.

Here are a few ways to kick you off:

Observe an unpleasant idea.

Focus on the feelings and substantial reactions that emerge.

Recognize that your feelings are valid for you at the time.

Receive an expression that addresses you, for example, "May I accept myself as I am" or "I am sufficient."

Grasp your fears

A few things will always be out of your control. Learning how to accept this can go far toward checking to overthink.

Obviously, this is not as easy as one might expect, and it won't occur incidentally. Be that as it may, search for little open doors where you can go up against the situations you, much of the time, stress over. Perhaps it's confronting a bossy associate or taking that independent day trip you've been longing for.

Request help

You don't need to go only to it. Looking for outside help from a certified specialist can assist you with growing new instruments for working through your thoughts and, in any event, changing your outlook.

Chapter 4:
What is a Highly Sensitive Person (HSP)?

Are you thinking about whether you are a highly sensitive individual? It is very conceivable that you really are. This fact may be influencing your association with worry in your life. Individuals who are considered to be "highly sensitive people" tend to feel things more profoundly than others, identify life's subtleties all the more effectively, and be progressively receptive to stimuli both inward and outside. They are people who might be progressively annoyed by a bothersome shirt or a rough friend. They are additionally people who will see when somebody needs an embrace or identify when something awful is going to occur and change course.

"The Highly Sensitive Person," HSP began to understand that there is nothing wrong with them. They simply have a superior tuned sensory system. Around 15–20% of the populace are HSP and have issues screening out stimuli and are overpowered by clamor and crowds.

"It means you know about subtleties in your environment, an extraordinary preferred position much of the time. It likewise means you are all the more effectively overpowered.

Signs that you're an HSP may include:

- You have been marked, sooner or later, excessively sensitive, shy, or introverted.
- You get depleted by crowds and need time alone to resuscitate yourself.

- You're sensitive to boisterous or monotonous commotions. Relentless talkers can overpower you.
- You have synthetic sensitivities or low resilience for scratchy garments.
- You're apprehensive about turning out to be choked by personal connections.
- You tend to socially detach yourself.
- You renew yourself in nature.
- You need quite a while to recover subsequent to being with troublesome people ("energy vampires").
- You favor balanced communications and little gatherings as opposed to huge social affairs.
- You flee from conflict. As an HSP, you feel the pressure and difference in a relationship profoundly, and numerous HSP report feeling physically sick during conflicts. This may make an HSP so conflict-avoidant that they will do anything to keep the other individual upbeat. This is on the grounds that conflict harms to such an extent. We can detect it is coming and experience the feelings of the other individual just as our own.
- You're sensitive to torment, impacts of caffeine, and brutal films. HSPs are frequently progressively sensitive to a wide range of torments, headaches, wounds, and so forth than non-HSP.
- You're incredibly awkward by brilliant lights, solid scents, and changes in your life.
- You're often genuinely depleted from engrossing others' feelings. Like an empath, an HSP going into a room may promptly detect the temperaments of the people in. This is again due to the fact that HSP is increasingly reasonable to subtleties — outward appearances, body language, manner of speaking, and in any event, breathing mood. Accordingly, HSPs may end up handling

feelings that are not their very own and, in this manner, experience the ill effects of regular passionate weariness.

- You need a lot of downtimes. Toward the end of a bustling day, you'll frequently wind up pulling back to a calm, obscured space to energize your batteries by bringing down your stimulation level.
- You have a high "frighten reflex."
- You're misconstrued. You end up mislabeled as being introverted or shy, and this may be on the grounds that HSP and introverts share numerous qualities, for example, requiring a ton of downtime.

Every HSP may be extraordinary, however. Some might be troubled uniquely by scents and can block out clamors. Others may just discover bright lights, unfortunately.

The Characteristics of a Highly Sensitive Person: All highly sensitive people (HSP) are one of a kind people, yet they share certain traits for all intents and purpose. An analyst who represents considerable authority in the point has built up an abbreviation that abridges them: DOES.

D: Depth of handling "HSP basically process everything more, relating and contrasting what they notice with their past encounters," Aron clarifies. "At the point when we decide without knowing how we went to that decision, we call this instinct, and HSP has a decent — however not trustworthy! — instinct."

O: Overstimulation "What's overstimu-lating to every individual is extraordinary," says Bevin Niemann, who mentors HSP and self-distinguishes as highly sensitive. "It could be a commotion, bright lights, crowds, enthusiastic situations — the scratchy labels in the rear of a shirt may be horrendous."

E: Emotional reactivity and compassion "We associate profoundly with the workmanship, music, theater, nature, creatures, stories, and books," Niemann says. Studies have seen HSP as particularly compassionate to other people, sometimes to the point of being overgiving.

S: Sensing the unobtrusive Highly sensitive people are receptive to signals that others may miss, Aron, affirms. "Our consciousness of subtleties is valuable in various ways, from basic joy in life to strategizing our reactions dependent on others' nonverbal signs."

By all appearances, Lynelle Trigalet was flourishing. In her mid-40s, she dealt with the frenzied ensemble look for an auditorium organization, where she directed groups of up to 30 workers. When she left the shop in the nights, be that as it may, things transformed: She had little energy for the remainder of her life. She'd make supper and afterward very quickly nod off before the TV. Her better half-kidded that she had an on/off switch.

Trigalet asked why she didn't appear to have as a lot of energy as others. Accepting the issue was her long work hours, she quit her place of employment to -become a health mentor. In any case, something was as yet not right. Her life — plus her marriage — was self-destructing, and she felt like "a failure in each perspective."

Wanting to switch vocations once more, Trigalet enrolled the assistance of an expert coach, who happened to inquire as to whether she was a "highly sensitive individual" or HSP. Trigalet scored high — "truly elevated," she says — and her underlying response to the mark was a disgrace. In the same way as other people, she related "sensitive" to being frail or excessively passionate.

In any case, HSP isn't just weary or psychotic. Highly sensitive people — an assignment that incorporates around 20 percent of the populace — have particularly responsive sensory systems. The attribute runs in families and even shows up in creature conduct.

These sorts make some harder memories sifting through possibly superfluous data, so their brains retain everything. They might be hypersensitive to sounds, bright lights, tastes, and scents, which means they get overstimulated effectively. In any case, these people are additionally frequently highly inventive, thorough, and fit for blending various data in novel ways.

Once Trigalet acknowledged that HSP, life events that had come to naught before, such as the fact that she cried every day during high school, made sense. She had never been depressed; I was tired and excited to interact with people all day.

The reason for his exhaustion after work also became apparent. Because HSP brains absorb so much information, they need extra interruption to process it. When she was busy managing her equipment, usually working at lunch, Trigalet had no downtime.

His whole life improved when he finally began to understand the trait he had used since birth. Their marriage stabilized when she and her partner recognized the reasons for their need for space and peace. And instead of struggling to be "different" and struggling to find a job that seems right for him, Trigalet used his astute and conscientious nature (another hallmark of HSP) to become a transformational leadership coach primarily working with HSP.

Framing past events and recognizing one's strengths is one of the key steps to flourishing as a sensitive person, says Aaron.

These strategies can help you support HSP, either yourself or a loved one.

Mental Self-Care

HSPs are often confused with introverts. Another blanket, but not the same. Aaron estimates that 70% of HSPs are introverts and 30% are extroverts. While this may seem more feminine in nature, the line also appears in women and men.

Similarly, many HSPs are considered shy or socially awkward when they are children, but they may not be at all. Sensitive people just need a little more time to process, said HSP coach and mentor. "We review the experience database. We approach models, test ideas, and then unify them."

If a sensitive individual is brought up in a culture that regards redundancy and sensitivity as a weakness, it can lead to feelings of inadequacy. But rethinking past experiences can help HSP understand the inconvenience of the past and move forward confidently.

Trigalet reassessed her teenage tears and the exhaustion of adults, teaching them to regard them as products of her sensitivity, not a lack of personality; The HSP could do the same and feel a greater sense of self-acceptance.

If your mind is being very sensitive: Leave room for a sensitive person during the break, a great way to show your support. You can also try to be patient while it takes your friend or loved one a little more time to process the information.

Physical Self-Care

An HSP finds the quality helpful for his training. "It's easy to instinctively pick up on various registers of feelings, practically like a decent performer figure out how to follow the unpredictable interchange of cacophony and consonance inside a melody. You're ready to see better degrees."

To oblige his affectability, for instance. "I realized those bright lights would be blasting in my face the entire day," he says. "By evolving them, I could be increasingly present and in this way progressively helpful."

Highly sensitive people frequently benefit from making little comparative modifications to their work environments and timetables, for example, considerately mentioning that a partner wears less scent or looking for authorization to take a fast snooze after lunch.

Standard dinners are likewise significant, as indicated by a specialist. Since low glucose levels can start tactile over-burden, it's helpful for these sorts to abstain from getting excessively ravenous.

At last, any kind of delicate development — yoga, long strolls in nature, bicycle rides — can give HSP an opportunity to physically scatter restless -energy without causing overstimulation.

If somebody you care about is highly sensitive: Managers, guardians, and others in supervisory positions can benefit from realizing that sensitive kinds work best when offered some calm downtime. Rest is vital for HSP — it enables them to recoup from such stimulation — and on the grounds that many are inclined to a sleeping disorder or intruded on rest, naps are particularly valuable.

Emotional Self-Care

HSP has extraordinary feelings — a ton of them.

They display exceptional compassion, frequently detecting the emotions and requirements of everyone around them (which can make them slip into an off-putting "fix it" mode). Their sometimes-permeable individual limits can exhibit a genuine test to friends and family, who may feel disregarded or may unwittingly misuse those caretaking tendencies.

This means creating solid limits is particularly key to their passionate wellbeing.

"HSP can pick up on things that are going on with others, and it's a significant workmanship to have the option to state, 'This is theirs; this is mine.' Just on the grounds that you can be open doesn't imply that you must be."

Great limits resemble a decent jazz organization, he says. "I have to return to my own instrument and make sure that I am in order and ability to 'read the progressions' before I attempt to make music with others."

Work on defining limits by saying no, beginning with easy communications. Calls, you can rehearse by saying, 'Kindly don't call me once more' and afterward hanging up.

"You don't need to make it into a major, long clarification when you set a limit," she includes. "'No' is a finished sentence."

For HSP who tend to feel the emotions of others, " Differentiating -between one's own emotions and those of another is an important expertise that gets simpler after some time, however sufficiently having attention to rehash a mantra is a basic initial step.

If somebody you care about is highly sensitive: When you cooperate with sensitive people, do whatever it takes not to think about it literally when they state no or set limits in different ways. Recollect that it's hard for them as far as possible, so as opposed to being frustrated or irritated by their cumbersomeness, you should think about praising their fearlessness.

Social Self-Care

Get-togethers (particularly parties) can be a test for highly sensitive sorts. The stimulation of a boisterous swarmed place is probably not going to draw out their best, and on the grounds that they tend toward profound thought, casual banter can be depleting. In a perfect world, HSPs will design a lot of downtimes, both when gathering encounters.

There are different advances they can take to make these social affairs progressively enjoyable. "Get ready ahead of time," recommends Jacquelyn Strickland, LPC, who directs HSP. "Get a satisfactory rest. Wear agreeable garments. Eat a little protein feast before you go."

Occasionally venturing outside or withdrawing to the restroom can help diminish tactile over-burden, and breathing activities will enhance a break's quieting impact. Inhale for a count of eight, holding it for a count of four, and afterward breathing out for a count of eight. Or then again, simply close your eyes, inhale profoundly, and block out extra stimuli.

If somebody you care about is highly sensitive: When attending a gathering with a highly sensitive friend, be set up to leave somewhat sooner than you may like; HSP will arrive at their immersion point sooner than most. If you realize you'd prefer to remain late at a social event, think about making arrangements for independent transportation.

These proposals are, on the whole temporary, obviously. "The No. 1 thing for very sensitive individuals is to have a self-care plan that depends on what their identity is," Strickland notes. HSP may have numerous comparative traits, yet everyone has exceptional needs. With some acceptance and thinking ahead, those requirements don't need to be a weight. Appropriate self-care can change that affectability into a gift.

Take the Quiz: Find an assortment of tests and useful articles, just as a test to decide whether you're an HSP.

Guide For Highly Sensitive People

A very sensitive person is a person who is in tune with their environment. They are often intuitive and empathetic, have a vivid imagination, and can feel very overwhelmed by noise, chaos, and crowds. They may have problems integrating and are considered "too shy" or "too sensitive."

About 20% of the population is estimated to be very sensitive. Many object to the term "very sensitive" because it is often considered a bad thing. Some prefer terms as highly customized or very conscious, as these terms do not have a negative connotation as "too sensitive."

It can be difficult to understand or treat very sensitive people. I think it's because we don't really understand each other. Certainly, I have not worked most of my life. As we saw that we were different from others when we were adults, other people, especially our parents and family, did not know how to behave with us. A very sensitive person often tries to integrate but cannot, so he concludes that there must be something wrong with them. They often tell us things like "you're too sensitive,"; "Overcome,"; "you're childish, growing up,"; and my favorite, "don't be so stupid." As if we were saying that in certain situations, we feel uncomfortable or that we do not want to do certain things, it is simply difficult for us.

If you are very sensitive or know someone who is, these tips can help you better understand what it means:

1. We're not sensitive. Being sensitive essentially implies that we are more fixed on the earth and on the people around us. We pick up on some things that most others don't. We notice things. It doesn't imply that we will self-destruct If you are immediate and legit with us (in fact, we favor it since then we know where we remain with you).
2. There's nothing wrong with us. We are not broken. We needn't bother with fixing. We are simply unique. We don't frequently enjoy very similar things that numerous others enjoy - and this isn't simply in our heads; it's a physical thing. We really feel physical indications that are awkward because of things like commotion, fluorescent lighting, smoke, aromas, concoction smells, swarms, clamorous conditions, etc.
3. We are not unsociable, nor show improvement over every other person. The individuals who are highly sensitive and furthermore introverts can react to over-stimulation by pulling back and getting peaceful. We may decrease to go along with you at a bar or an occasion where there are bunches of people, not on the grounds that we're unsociable, but since we realize we wouldn't enjoy it, and we would endure a while later. We all know, in reality, that it can take us days to recuperate from such over-stimulation.
4. Not every highly sensitive person is an introvert and the other way around. There are people who are outgoing but then likewise highly sensitive. The thing that

matters is that a contemplative HSP will tend to pull back when encountering over-stimulation, while a social butterfly may lash out and get forceful or furious. Albeit once more, this relies upon the individual, and not all outgoing HSP will act along these lines.

5. It's easy to feel that HSP probably won't thrive in initiative positions. The inverse is valid. They can thrive (Despite the fact that they may not always need to). In fact, HSP makes incredible pioneers since they can be more in line with different colleagues who have a more extensive point of view. They likewise tend to pick up on things that others may miss -, for example, feelings, body language, outward appearances - on the grounds that they are so highly mindful.
6. There's no uncertainty about it; being highly sensitive can be troublesome. Be that as it may, those troubles are significantly decreased, and your sensitivities can be turned into incredible qualities once you completely comprehend and claim what your identity is. It's easy to presume there must be something wrong with you when you are not equivalent to most others. Be that as it may, being diverse isn't an issue. It's a blessing. Realize what your identity is and while testing situations come up, help other people to comprehend. Don't anticipate that they should naturally know, and you should support them and realize how to support yourself.

While there are major differences between very sensitive people (HSP), we have one thing in common: HSP has a sensitive nervous system that has the filtration of the difficult and the easier to overcome in our environment.

Often, most societies believe that their emotional HSPs are sensitive, reactive, withdrawn, or linguistic, which is a wrong assumption. But if it is clear from the beginning, the HSP may even face an unfavorable environment if necessary.

Chapter 5: Ways to Cope With Stress If You are Highly Sensitive

Set limits

When we talk about "borders," we mean limitations in your relationships,

but we think about it in other ways. This means that you feel more comfortable so that people know where you are and what you need: classic restriction techniques. But we also refer to things like creating extra flexibility in your schedule so that you do not feel stressed when things inevitably go wrong, pile up, or seek an additional response from your own side.

Practice meditation and mindfulness.

These practices are closely similar to the idea of setting limits. This is because these feelings create a circle around their life experiences and their thoughts and feelings towards them through practices of meditation and mindfulness.

When you make use of meditation, first step back and observe your thoughts and feelings, and even your physical reactions are separate from your life and your "I." With practice, some important things happen. Learn to calm your body faster by reversing your stress response and return to a calm place. You also learn to detach yourself emotionally, so if things seem superfluous to you, you will not be so easily overwhelmed during the emotions. It helps you stay grounded, and it can also help you develop your resilience to stress. All of this should be worth it to everyone, but this is especially true of a very sensitive person.

"Areas of relaxation" for you

This can mean that your home is quiet and relatively conflict-free. This can be achieved by adding some things that are known to relieve stress, such as relaxing music and aromatherapy, and regular "breaks."

It can also mean that you maintain as close a relationship as possible. This can be achieved by learning conflict resolution and assertiveness techniques, which can provide you with the tools you need to defeat the difficulties that may arise between you and your loved ones.

Finally, it also means that you can choose to have the people in your life in your inner circle after spending on dignity, and you can put a distance between yourself and those who empty you. Frustrate or devalue When you have a circle of people who will listen to you and take care of you when you have difficulties in life, you can be even calmer if you are sensitive; Sensitive people require to feel understood and supported a little more than others, and they are also wonderful in their ability to offer this in return. But it is important to maintain your support for those who will return it, at least in part, instead of those who will exhaust it and abandon it or raise self-doubt.

Self Care Practice

As a very sensitive person, you are probably more sensitive to the devastation of sleep deprivation, poor diet, and exhaustion. This means that you should get enough sleep at night (or drink as needed), eat healthy meals, and take proper care of your body, mind, and spirit in every way possible. This will allow you to manage better what comes your way.

Know your triggers

All very sensitive people have their own challenges. It is helpful to know what attracts you most to avoid such things in your life. Take note of how you feel all day and even keep a stress log if needed. Be proactive in adding resilience-building practices as well as removing stressors as much as possible.

You may have little or no power to change the fact that you are a sensitive person, although you can absolutely change your lifestyle and habits by being less sensitive to stressors, you cannot control. With some time, it will become second nature, and you will feel more resilient to stress in general. Then you can enjoy the benefits of sensitivity.

HSPs Tend to Fail to Use Certain Strategies

As it occurs, a research paper was simply distributed specifying, "Is the connection between tangible preparing affectability and negative impact interceded by emotional regulation?"

Initially, reliable with other research, these researchers found that HSP is increasingly aware of and has progressively negative emotions–depression, anxiety, feeling stressed–than others. Second, this will assist you with getting the significant finding for you, that among numerous strategies that assist everybody with controlling and accordingly diminish their negative emotions, HSP tends to do certain ones less. Thus, If you need to help your emotional regulation, increment these five:

1. Accept your feelings.

2. Do not be ashamed of them.
3. Believe you can adapt just as others do.
4. Trust that your terrible feelings won't keep going long.
5. Assume there's hope–you can take care of your awful feelings in the end.

Why there Might be Trouble with these Five

A colossal factor raising HSP to have ruckus with these five, as the researchers found, is that we just are increasingly aware of negative feelings (everything being equal, yet they didn't gauge positive ones). Maybe a few of us have had such a large number of awful encounters that the run of the mill strategies don't work. Possibly our negative feelings do last a more drawn out time, dang it, and we can't change them! Possibly these "frames of mind" are exactly how it is for a few of us, particularly the individuals who didn't learn regulation strategies while youthful. The researchers didn't take a gander at the impact of the historical backdrop of past negative encounters, particularly in youth, or the work one has done to mend these. If that had been considered, there might have been a little relationship between negative impact, particularly depression, and being an HSP.

Then again, HSP tends to be higher on most proportions of anxiety and being stressed, given the idea of the inquiries. Whatever our past, we stress (and cheer and feel appreciation) more than others, and a considerable lot of us are stressed by attempting to oversee a non-HSP world. All things considered, we can apply the over five to anxiety and feeling stressed.

This isn't Your Fault, yet There Are Things You Can Do frequently The failure to utilize those five is, once more, at any rate from the outset oblivious. So you may need to perceive these first—for instance, that you are ashamed of your negative feelings or you can't help suspecting that they will go on for eternity. So maybe simply perusing this will make these dispositions progressively cognizant and accessible for you to change. In particular, obviously, it replaces a feeling of destruction with a little hope and certainty when searching for and applying new strategies. Maybe the best spot to start is talking explicitly to other HSP who have genuinely battled at this point found answers. Thus our other blog entry today, by a friend and partner, an HS will locate his own horrendously significant way through his lifelong depression and anxiety.

Most importantly, emotional regulation can be learned. You can begin with self-improvement, except if you are having self-destructive thoughts. At that point, you need assistance immediately. Beginning there, at the outrageous, one approach to controlling emotions that we regularly overlook is through meds—it's truly alright If you have to and endure them. Simply find a specialist who is thoughtful and sees high affectability, at any rate, when you clarify it. Another approach to begin is to see a decent psychotherapist acquainted with HSP, who will assist you with finding the best procedure for directing your emotions, and if the initial ones don't work, assist you with investigating why and find new ones.

An HSP feels their emotions all the more firmly, HSP ponders things all the more profoundly, and sometimes goes to insane places in their minds. These emotions can help or damage your business, and in an excessive number of cases, it is a significant issue. Here are six emotions that should always be checked If you are a highly sensitive person and entrepreneur.

1. Jealousy.

The word reference characterizes jealousy as "feelings of stress over the potential loss of something important." In business, encountering jealousy is genuinely normal; however, those feelings are enhanced when you're a highly sensitive person. You are apprehensive and experience minutes that undermine your business as you make up situations in your mind.

Whenever left unchecked, jealousy can possibly derail advance or much more dreadful. As an HSP, you need to assess the situation soundly. This may mean talking it over with a care group, for example, a mastermind gathering—or thinking about things unbiasedly. Get to the reason for why the jealousy is in your mind and manage it before it rots.

2. Envy.

Jealousy and envy are frequently confounded. Envy is a feeling of discontent or disdain for what another person has. This may be one of the most widely recognized feelings in niche businesses. Envy feels too incredible for a highly sensitive person to even think about overcoming. We see another person's prosperity and let our jealous thoughts divert us from what we ought to do.

Your focus, as an entrepreneur, ought to be what the following stages are that will enable your business to develop. Online life has permitted us access such that makes envy a typical feeling. Because an entrepreneur had achievement doesn't imply that what they did is directly for your business. You can not envy what they've done or had, and you need to make this about those your business serves. This can't exclusively be about you. If you battle with envy, realize that it is a feeling and feeling you can overcome with the best possible viewpoint and focus.

3. Anger.

Blowing up is a part of being human. In the case of a highly sensitive person, we feel anger in an unexpected way. We go crazy in a baffling situation and spend additional time than we should allow that anger. Before we know it, a little issue turns into a life-evolving occasion. Anger will undoubtedly occur, yet it shouldn't be a feeling that influences your business. Work it out, address the motivation behind why you're frantic, and don't allow it to assemble. Discharging is your most obvious opportunity as a highly sensitive person.

4. Anxiety.

Feeling apprehensive and on edge is basic for highly sensitive people. Entrepreneurs, when all is said in done, experience these emotions every once in a while. It's normal to feel anxiety with specific decisions, yet it shouldn't injure you from doing what should be done while performing your business operations. If you consider yourself to be a highly sensitive person, anxiety can hurt you. Much the same as different emotions, get to the underlying driver, and take care of business.

5. Impulsiveness.

At the point when an HSP needs something, we need it immediately. We see another showcasing strategy or procedure that we think will grow our business, and we act before thinking it through. Being impulsive never converts into a keen technique for any entrepreneur. Arranging, thinking, guidance, and more are important to encounter success in business.

6. Satisfaction.

Feeling content about your life or business isn't really an awful thing. In any case, for a highly sensitive person, being too content means agreeing to be short of what we need. Satisfaction prompts comfort, and an excessive amount of comfort causes a lack of concern. In order for your business endeavors to flourish, you have to grow as a person, and you can't do that in case you're excessively comfortable with any success you've just experienced. Be upbeat and thankful for what you have; a demeanor of appreciation is incredible; however, always endeavor to arrive at greater and more elevated levels of success.

Being a highly sensitive person does not render you less of an entrepreneur. It means that you feel emotions in an alternate manner; however, you can utilize that to further your potential benefit. You can feel for your clients and business all the more profoundly, and that will make a more profound association.

What Highly Sensitive People Should Consider to Be Happy

1. A slower, less difficult pace of life

Since they process data profoundly, HSPs may move a little slower than non-HSPs. They may require more opportunity to carry out specific responsibilities, such as escaping the house in the first part of the day. They may take somewhat longer to make decisions, for example, which thing to purchase at the market, since they are taking in the pile of decisions, yet in addition nourishment data, cost, and how they feel about chicken noodle.

2. Time to slow down following a busy day

Like introverts, HSP can't go-go-go for a really long time. Their additional sensitive sensory systems ingest hills of data and procedure it to the umpteenth degree. Subsequently, they may get easily overpowered and exhausted following a busy day. Time to loosen up brings down their stimulation level and reestablishes their mental soundness.

3. A quiet, calm space to withdraw to

Ideally, #2 is matched with #3. This space, in a perfect world, would have low lighting, little clamor, a warm feeling, a lovely look, and the HSP's preferred instruments to unwind (a book, music, a comfortable pad, and so forth.).

4. Consent to get emotional and have a decent cry

Not exclusively are HSPs additional sensitive to ecological stimulation; they're likewise sensitive emotionally. "Sensitive people can't resist the urge to express what they're feeling," "They show their anger, they show their satisfaction. Valuing that is extremely significant."

5. Time to conform to change

Advances can be extreme for anybody, yet for HSPs, they can rapidly snowball into a heap of pressure and overpower. Indeed, even positive changes, such as beginning another relationship or moving into a fantasy home, can be overstimulating and require an extra extensive stretch of modification.

6. Close, important connections

HSPs ache for profound associations with others. In fact, as indicated by Aron, they may get exhausted or eager to see someone that needs an important connection. Nonetheless, this doesn't imply that they're inclined to relationship bouncing. Or maybe, they may really work more enthusiastically to start up a significant discussion with their partner and make closeness.

Chapter 6:
Building Mental Toughness

Mental toughness is a quite common term that has been for quite some time discussed yet regularly misconstrued. Luckily, in the previous 12 years, researchers have started to examine this wonder. Despite the fact that there are contrasts among researchers, mental toughness seems to contain four basic attributes, including motivation, coping with pressure, focus, and confidence. As far as creating mental toughness, one approach to move toward its advancement is to think that it is sometimes educated and sometimes gotten. Instructing mental toughness includes a conscious endeavor to prepare explicit mental abilities (e.g., objective setting, unwinding, focus) though sometimes mental toughness is basically gotten because of environmental impacts (e.g., having kin how was more seasoned yet pushed you to be progressively aggressive and to endeavor to improve persistently). The research closes with certain recommendations for future research, remembering focusing on the early improvement of mental toughness just as creating mediations to test the viability of

Grasp what your identity is and utilize that to help your business grow mental toughness preparing.

Pillars of Mental Toughness As simply noted, albeit different models and frameworks of mental toughness have been created, given a valuable, useful framework dependent on the attributes of mental toughness look into that arranges the different attributes into the four pillars of mental toughness (i.e., motivation, self-assurance, attentional focus, coping with pressure). From a viable point of view, the pillars of mental toughness can give an organized framework to which to identify strategies to instruct and build mental toughness.

The four pillars are depicted underneath and are later used to offer down-to-earth strategies on the best way to build mental toughness by either showing mental aptitudes or making a reasonable situation (e.g., physical, mental, emotional, social).

Motivation

Perceiving that particular types of motivation and motivational strategies are more favorable than others for ideal execution, this column is fixated on the ideal levels and types of motivation required to achieve your goals. The motivation for the mentally tough athlete would incorporate a powerful urge for success; eagerness to propel oneself, continue, and work hard; defining troublesome however feasible goals, and skipping once again from execution difficulties.

Fearlessness is viewed as one of the most significant mental toughness qualities, and this column typifies mentally tough athletes' conviction that they have the capacities to achieve their goals. This solid confidence in oneself empowers the mentally tough athlete to go out on a limb, learn from analysis, control undesirable thoughts and feelings, and expect that beneficial things will occur later on, for instance.

Attentional Focus

Having the option to focus their attention on the important prompts in the environment and keep up that focus in spite of interruptions, just as not enabling things to reduce their attention from their needs, is a sign of mentally tough athletes. Mentally tough athletes keep up such attentional focus by focusing on controlling the controllable; remaining at the time; focusing on the positives, and focusing on the procedure.

Coping with pressure

This column identifies with having the option to perform under tension by controlling the sum and nature of stress experienced. The various parts of pressure as it identifies with mental toughness incorporate coping successfully with affliction; remaining quiet under tension; accepting that anxiety is unavoidable and enjoying it; flourishing with pressure, and translating anxiety as facilitative for execution.

Creating Mental Toughness

Although there are on-going exploration and discussion as to precisely how mental toughness is developed, from an existing examination, apparently mental toughness is both "gotten" by means of environmental influences and "instructed" through preparing, following a comparative line of request to ability development, mental toughness researchers have utilized the intelligent accounts of tip-top athletes to give significant data on how they developed their mental toughness during prior phases of their careers.

Findings from these examinations feature that mental toughness can be developed (i.e., got) through certain environmental influences. For instance, environmental influences gave the foundation to the development of tough character (e.g., aggressiveness), tough dispositions (e.g., go the additional mile mindset), and tough thinking (e.g., strong fearlessness) in tip-top cricketers. When talking about environmental influences, athletes who are reflectively reviewing their development are not referring to situations that they have intentionally set themselves in to build up their mental toughness independently. In any case, rather, they review how the environment has impacted them.

Chapter 7: How to Develop Mental Toughness:

The Roles of Parents and Coaches

Coaches and parents have significant tasks to carry out in creating mental toughness (regardless of whether "got" or "instructed"). In an investigation focusing on the National Collegiate Athletic Association (NCAA) athletes, for instance, coaches were accounted for as having the most impact in building up their mental toughness. These strategies included making a tough physical practice environment (e.g., extraordinary aggressive practices, tough physical conditioning), a non-negative but positive mental environment (e.g., confidence building/positive air, elevated standards), and giving awareness/learning openings (e.g., watching others being mentally tough). Essentially, in an examination including athletes' mental toughness development crosswise over career stages, coaches were referenced as being significant in the development of mental toughness, explicitly referring on numerous occasions to the coaches' administration styles. Basically, coaches were viewed as legitimately (tutoring, arranged educating) or by implication (encouraging/supporting/imparting significant aptitudes) showing mental abilities. Executing tough physical conditioning is developing in writing as one approach to build a tough practice environment. For instance, NCAA coaches announced utilizing tough physical conditioning to build the mental toughness attributes of performing under tension and self-belief. The degree to which mental toughness has a physical segment isn't completely comprehended, albeit a predictable finding is that being physically arranged is connected to showing significant levels of self-conviction. From a functional viewpoint, this association between the physical and mental angles ought to be accentuated when building.

Designing training, Sessions, and Mental toughness.

Controlling practice environments to make focused, difficult and pressure actuating situations is an important system for building mentally tough athletes. Notwithstanding, these environments should be positive and confidence-building instead of negative and discipline arranged. For instance, elite athletes have reported that being in a fulfilling (e.g., opportunity to show capacity) and enjoyable (e.g., an opportunity to ace skills) environment has influenced their mental toughness development and gives off an impression of being particularly notable in developing the motivational attributes. These findings are steady with the ability development, and with a great part of the ongoing game, brain research looks into fortification and feedback, which emphasizes a positive approach to the learning and performance of skills and competencies.

To create this positive atmosphere, coaches should consider providing fortification and feedback, which emphasizes a positive approach to learning and performing skills and competencies (e.g., provide support, provide positive and informative feedback, establish fun practices and be nice, think about individual contracts).

To develop mental toughness, athletes being presented to empowering environments (both inside and outside of the game setting) isn't just connected to the roles of coaches yet additionally to the roles of athletes' parents.

A predictable finding in youth-sport writing is that parents assume a focal job in their child's donning involvement with general and can likewise influence their motivation to participate in sport and their enjoyment. Ability development writing supports that parents are important in helping hopeful youthful athletes to satisfy their latent capacity and progress through the different phases of their careers.

The job of parents impacting a proper demeanor towards sport participation was found in ponders, including NCAA Division one athlete just as elite cricketers. The common subject among these exploration findings is that parents empowered an "if it's worth doing, it's worth doing right" mindset.

Altogether, these findings demonstrate that with fitting support and consolation, parents can influence the development of mental toughness. It is necessary to take note of that current game brain research writing in these zones (e.g., mental toughness, mental ability development, youth sport) regularly recognizes that parents ought to receive a proper degree of contribution in their child's game development to be supportive. In particular, parents keeping up a fitting point of view on their child's donning inclusion, empowering possession, and duty, just as being part of a supportive social support network, are viewed as important parent practices for developing elite athletes' mental qualities and mental toughness.

Preparing to be Mentally Tough: Combining "Educated" and "Got" Strategies notwithstanding controlling the preparation environment to develop mental toughness as recently examined (i.e., the got component), mental skills seem to have an important task to carry out in preparing athletes to be mentally tough. To drive home this view, elite athletes have reported the successful utilization of mental skills (e.g., mental readiness, symbolism, objective setting, self-talk) in helping them not exclusively to develop their mental toughness yet additionally as a methodology to look after it. Mediation explores given primer support to the helpfulness of mental skills, preparing to focus on explicit mental toughness attributes for its improvement with youth footballers. While actualizing strategies to develop mental toughness, both information from environmental influences and explicit mental skills can be consolidated for ideal adequacy. Utilizing the four pillars of the mental toughness model as a framework, the following area draws upon the development of mental toughness writing to give a diagram of certain strategies to build mental toughness.

Motivation

The desire to succeed and maintain this intrinsic motivation over long periods are often considered essential qualities of mental strength. This desire can be driven by intrinsic and extrinsic motivation, although research has shown that people with strong intrinsic motivation show more interest, enthusiasm, confidence, and persistence than people with the most motivation for external requirements and rewards.

Create an effective environment.

Coaches can create a coaching environment where athletes are exposed to successful experiences. With that in mind, they can focus not only on the outcome but also on the fun and can engage in certain decisions to create a sense of ownership. With regard to the practice environment, although a positive motivational climate seems to be appropriate to enhance intrinsic motivation, the use of competitive rivalry in the development of motivational properties of mental strength has received some support in the literature. In addition, creating a difficult environment by applying intense competitive practices was mentioned by all the coaches he spoke with as a strategy for developing mentally difficult athletes. In particular, coaches designed the exercises "to put athletes in difficult situations and encourage them to stick." In addition to the training environment, it is also important to keep in mind that the behaviors that coaches adopt can play an important role in the development of an athlete's intrinsic motivation. For example, coaches can focus on offering rewards to athletes who depend on their performance, using verbal and non-verbal compliments and the ability to change the content and exercise order.

Training motivation

The strategy of setting mental goals can be used to improve the motivational properties of mental strength. For example, elite athletes from a study in Connaughton stated that goal-setting was a key skill used in their mental preparation and helped them develop their inner desire and motivation to succeed. In general, research has shown that goals focus attention and action and help players focus on what they should be doing in the short and long term. Having certain goals to achieve the desired results is considered more effective than setting goals "give your best" or simply knowing what you want (for example, winning a championship). In fact, the results of objective research consistently show that specific and difficult goals achieve better performance than easy goals, for your best goals or not at all. According to some scientific literature, a goal is generally defined as a goal, standard, goal, or degree of performance or competence, and there are three main types of goals, namely results, goals, and process goals.

The definition of each type of goal can improve athletic performance, although research with elite athletes has shown that a combination of these three types of goals is associated with optimal performance. When considering the types of goals to be identified as athletes, it is important that for each outcome goal there must be several performance goals and establish processes that ultimately lead to that outcome. Existing literature points out that mentally hard-working athletes not only clearly focus on their long-term goals, but can also control their concentration at important times during the competition. In addition to the types of goals, certain key principles are involved in defining effective goals. Good advice to help athletes remember the principles of effective goals is S.M.A.R.T.S.

Self-belief; Existing literature reliably supports self-belief as a key attribute of mental toughness, with some positioning this feature as the most important. Self-belief identifies with an athlete's confidence, and various examinations have uncovered that confidence positively affects sports performance. Likewise, confidence is considered one of the most important attributes an athlete can have, yet it is also considered as one of the most delicate attributes. In this way, finding ways to build and keep up confidence is important for mental toughness development and for successful performance.

Creating a compelling environment: The importance of creating an authority and positive motivational atmosphere has emerged in mental toughness development. In revealing some insight into developmental contemplations, athletes' memories of developing mental toughness attributes, for example, self-belief, desire, and thought processes to prevail all through differing career stages (i.e., early, center, later) included authority, enjoyment, presentation to friendly contentions, and social support. In a later report, coaches stressed that building confidence in athletes needed a positive environment and loads of help (e.g., consolation, positive and instructional feedback Research has additionally featured the job that physical arrangement can play when developing the confidence part of mental toughness. In particular, quality physical readiness is frequently linked with positive mental attributes, for example, confidence. Along these lines, with self-belief being reported as the most important attribute of mental toughness in different examinations, it isn't astonishing that being completely arranged physically has emerged in writing as a potential essential to exhibiting explicit attributes of mental toughness, for example, confidence and performing under tension.

Preparing self-belief Based on flow, mental toughness look into, upgrading self-belief has all the earmarks of being linked with strategies, for example, displaying/watching others, and reviewing past successful activities.

Mental toughness: what exactly is mental toughness and how to build it; bearing witness to its positive impact in improving performance, yet additionally upgrading mental skills. So far in the mental toughness writing, athletes have reported utilizing imagery for an assortment of reasons, including remaining focused, building self-belief, and expanding their desire to achieve goals. When cultivating the self-belief aspect of mental toughness, it is important for coaches to perceive the incentive in giving athletes chances to watch their own performances and late achievements yet in addition to watch other successful athletes. The utilization of video clasps and performance examination can be joined into athletes' practice timetables to encourage this development. Coaches can likewise join imagery into their practice environments to help athletes mentally get ready for competition. For instance, coaches can get out various plays to their particular units whereby the players are then approached to envision what they would do in explicit situations.

Another technique may be for coaches to request that their players picture their occasions the prior night competition and see themselves completing the developments and strategies as required. Presumably, one of the most important employment of imagery would picture positive performances as an approach to build a vigorous self-belief. Reviewing a positive performance can assist athletes in keeping up the confidence to perform explicit skills during the competition. Attentional control Concentration is the capacity to stay focused on the task at hand and keep up that focus over some stretch of time. Having the option to remain completely focused, particularly when looked at with difficulty, is reliably reported as an important mental toughness attribute. Notwithstanding elite athletes perceiving the importance of focus for mental toughness, coaches additionally believe it to be an important attribute. The focal subject is that paying little respect to what is happening in the environment, mentally tough athletes have solid attentional control skills and can focus on the task at hand.

Creating a viable environment: The practice environment when learning mental skills is similarly as important as the learning of physical skills. To improve fixation in competition, it is important that attentional control is self-checked (e.g., observing how much time was spent on a given task or identifying situations when you had great focus as opposed to losing focus) and that competition is mimicked during practice. With respect to the development of fixation, setting up practices that urge athletes to make speedy decisions is one approach to prepare focus. In addition, over-learning skills in practice can empower athletes to make entangled decisions rapidly during competition. Lastly, the mentor can "pause" or "freeze play" during training to ask players what they are focusing on while performing a particular task. By doing this prep work, players can get quick feedback on what they are focusing on and how they can improve it.

Preparing attentional control: Although numerous strategies have been recognized to improve attention control (e.g., competition designs and built up schedules, negative idea stopping), ongoing exploration supports the utility of self-talk explanations. Two regular reasons for attentional issues tend to be as inside distracters, for example, attending to past occasions) or attending to future occasions. In this manner, developing a lot of specific verbal and positive prompts can assist athletes in keeping their minds focused on a given task. Verbal signs tend to be separated into either motivational (e.g., I can do it) or instructional (e.g., watch out for the ball) and can both be proper depending upon the situation. For mental toughness development, instructional self-talk gives specific data on the best way to perform an ability, though motivational self-talk can assist athletes with accomplishing their ideal prepared state competition or help them to hold tight during tough competition.

Managing pressure, a steady topic when examining mental toughness, is the players' capacity to deal with their emotions and cope with pressure. Mentally tough athletes don't just manage pressure; however, they thrive on it and can create an outstanding performance at important minutes. It is important that athletes develop a scope of coping strategies since they will, without a doubt, experience an assortment of stressors all through their donning careers.

Creating a successful environment

Recent research into the development of mental strength throws light on how elite athletes have learned to control their anxiety and progress through certain pressures from afar. In particular, athletes felt that they had learned to cope with anxiety and pressure due to the experience of aggressive aggression. Therefore, it is important for the development of mental resilience for athletes to present themselves with specific stressors in a training environment so that they can learn to appreciate the pressure. While considering the best practice environment for mental toughness development, examine recommends that physical conditioning ought to be part of it. Different systems to cope with pressure can be utilized and coordinated into athletes' physical practice environments. For instance, coaches can make pressure situations in different ways and will frequently include controlling time, space, and levels of restriction (e.g., over-burden situations) inside the drills that reverberate a game-related situation. In addition, coaches can decide to hold a physical conditioning session toward the beginning of practice with the goal that players will be set up to perform skills when they feel exhausted. This approach would lend itself to how a few athletes and coaches in writing think about the job of wellness. That is, athletes would most likely just have the option to perform something 'breathtaking' under tension towards the end of the game If they were physically fit.

Training to manage pressure concerning athletes learning to accept anxiety as part of the competition, it is important that they are furnished with certain strategies to assist them with viewing anxiety as having to a greater degree a positive influence than a negative influence on performance. One important coping instrument to encourage a positive translation of cognitive anxiety that is supported in writing is cognitive restructuring. Cognitive restructuring can assist athletes with countering negative thoughts and expectations and turn them into positive thoughts and expectations through a procedure of justification.

Normally, 'countering' includes the accompanying three stages: (an) identifying negative thoughts and situations that trigger them through self-observing methodology, (b) developing an idea stopping promptly to help stop the negative thoughts before they become hurtful to performance, and (c) supplanting the negative thoughts with positive thoughts that can coordinate your focus back to the task at hand.

"I love training and building up my physique. This is something I have made an enormous part of my life for the previous five years, and I don't ever observe myself stopping. I've found energy that makes me upbeat, feel great, and I need to work more diligently in each part of life; however, most importantly, it has shown me mental toughness. A decent dominant part of you realizes that I lost my father to an auto collision eight years back. For some of the people that don't know, this was a tremendous misfortune for my family and me. This disaster left us mistook for what the future had come up for us. That day we lost our father was a day we lost a bit of our family, and we realized it could never be fixed. Despite the fact that I could have gotten lost in an outright flood and said, "F*%K life!" I went the contrary way and took my anger out in the weight room! Don't misunderstand me here, and I had a considerable amount of mistakes along this voyage; however, it wouldn't have made me the man that I am today without them.

This is the place my intensity and drive originates from, throughout each and every day in the gym and everything outside of the gym. This type of intensity that I've assembled has originated from anger, life encounters, tirelessness, mistakes, and training. This has all driven me to get mentally tough in life. I said to myself, "for what reason would I go to the gym five days per week, train my rear end off, and afterward be a pushover in life?" What to simply build my physique and look great? Damnation no! I, at that point, asked myself, "Is there any valid reason why I wouldn't matter this equivalent type of intensity that I have at the gym to everything outside of the gym?" That's the place everything clicked. My weight training would prompt mental toughness training, to say the very least. In this article, I'm not saying I will make you mentally tough, yet I guarantee I will make you consider many things, and I nearly promise you will need to practice some mental toughness training and truly see if you're tough where it really counts. Prepared, set, how about we go!

Nowadays, you can basically purchase anything you need (boobs, cars, garments, and so forth); however, you can't purchase confidence and mental toughness. This comes through difficult work and perseverance. This comes through rebuffing work, and with that, perseverance can be instructed. Mental toughness training isn't for everybody, except it ought to be. It's unquestionably required. Without mental toughness, you are always defenseless for a breakdown regardless of how huge you are or how good you look. Realizing you can overcome affliction is the best quality of all. The issue is there isn't an easy way or alternate way of showing mental toughness. Mental toughness isn't available to be purchased. It's not something that is given. The best way to grow mentally tougher is by winning it. Like any skills one builds, perseverance can be worked in, practiced, and fortified. Consider perseverance like a muscle. The more you work it, the more grounded it will get. If you don't utilize it, it will decay (shrivel). If this all sounds excessively dubious, consider perseverance your will.

We have to apply the quality that we have in the gym into mental quality in life and carry that over to each curveball life tosses at us. Your gym doesn't have the foggiest idea what sort of issues you are experiencing. Indeed, even probably the nearest people in your life don't understand either. Training your mind and body ought to go hand in hand. In case you're in the gym day by day, hitting it hard, and giving it everything you have, after you're done, you can't stay here and disclose to me you don't feel like a beast when you leave the gym to your car. With that equivalent repressed monster that was released in the gym and strolling to the car ought to be carried over to each perspective in life. A good case of this is with a standard workout, and people give up too easily on the grounds that it's not testing. During an intense workout, you're enacting your hormones (EPOC levels, GH, Testosterone), and you raise your agony resilience. With extraordinary hard workouts, you push yourself harder, and that is a similar way you should approach life. You ought not to become a pushover or return to latent mode. You carry that equivalent forceful mentality into your everyday life, regardless of what you do. I state this since what is the point in just having that feeling for 1-2 hours of your day? If you have that creature feeling at the gym and worked hard for it, at that point, you reserve that option to carry that recognition over to this present reality. Level Out! No inquiries posed!

Everybody wants to be mentally tougher; however, not every person wants to put in the work. The main issue that will decide whether you will turn out to be mentally more grounded is your determination. Along these lines, you need to always test yourself and perceive how determined you really are. The more determined your will is, the more uncertain you will give up. Probably the ideal way to practice invigorating your will is the point at which you work out. Get your will engaged with your workout; however much as could be expected. For instance, in case you're doing leg augmentations and are battling with the last reps, rather than feeling "the siphon" of your muscles, associate with your will. Perceive what number of more reps you get by mentally willing yourself to accomplish more. It's a slight distinction from what you as of now do. In any case, you need to give more credibility to your will for doing the hard stuff as opposed to your body parts. This type of practice will, in the end, demonstrate your will and determination, and overtime will prompt more noteworthy achievements inside and outside of the gym.

Your body and mind will mess around with you when you work out. Your mind is your most noticeably awful foe. It will search for ways to cut you down or not let you train. This is the place your will and determination become an integral factor. It is okay to say that you are mentally ready to tell your body, "Kiss my can" I'm working out regardless of how I feel, or I'm breaking out another rep regardless? Because your body is exhausted doesn't equate to that, your mind must be worn out. Will your body be forceful and steady in the face of fatigue. Learning to be mentally dynamic when your body is powerless is an indication of will! A case of this is the point at which I began a Russian-style training routine, and I would be hunching down, seating, squeezing, or deadlifting 2-3 times per week. My body was sore as heck, yet I tried my will and tested myself and eventually traversed the routine. I disposed of the man and released the beast that is within me. I genuinely accept everybody has this interior beast, and you simply need to learn how to enact it and use it appropriately.

Why we don't turn out to be mentally tough in personal life is a direct result of FEAR. Fear is a good thing; it ought to be an instrument for us and propel us to overcome adverse situations in life. That is the place fortitude originates from when we are assaulting things we fear. Along these lines, rather than being scared to attempt another workout or routine since you believe it's excessively testing or you physically can't do it. Attempt really testing yourself and escaping your comfort zone. You need to engage with being in uncomfortable situations and check whether you can overcome them. For instance, If you're scared of open talking, at that point, start rehearsing it more to overcome its fear. That is a genuine trial of beating an adverse situation and getting grit. Face your fears in life, escape your comfort zone, and see what you are genuinely made of.

We as a whole work our rear ends off at the gym so we can build incredible looking bodies and become as physically solid as could be allowed. Being mentally tougher can help carry over all the work you put in to improve your body and quality. More importantly, being mentally tough can help improve your personal satisfaction since it instructs you to overcome adverse situations. Honestly, that is the thing that life is good at, creating adverse difficulties for people. In any case, do you disintegrate? Or otherwise, you incline toward your will and overcome it? Life is about a progression of punches being tossed at us, and eventually, you will get knocked down. Indeed, even the incredible and best people get knocked down. However, it's dependent upon you to either remain down or get back up and continue swinging.

Learn to change antagonism into inspiration with something reachable and specific with a potential arrangement. We have to learn to change the negative idea designs into positive self-talk. For instance, rather than saying, "I can't do these five sets of squats. There's simply no chance I can physically do it." Say, "I'm getting mentally more grounded, and I will blast out these five sets, to say the very least!" Tell yourself this beforehand, whether it's in your mind or for all to hear. Who gives a crap what others think. When you have any little uncertainty or pessimism in your mind, you have just vanquished yourself, your will, and your determination. Condition your mind to OUTWORK!

So with regards to mental toughness training. I don't need you to believe it's a type of training that you can build up through sets and redundancies. It's a lot further than that, and it requires some investment, hard work, life encounters, and perseverance. You should see a relationship with your life and training to apply mental toughness training to your everyday life. Make certain to push yourselves, test your will, overcome affliction, never give up, outwork people, learn to change cynicism into energy, overcome uncomfortable situations and fear, become forceful in life and don't be a pushover, and carry that repressed monster that is at the gym over to this present reality, to say the least. Be MENTALLY TOUGH! Always remember, you are your most noticeably awful adversary! Harmony!

With regards to specific people, some are brought into the world mentally tough, and others are definitely not. Does this imply If you would one say one are of the people that aren't brought into the world mentally tough that you can never get tough? The appropriate response is no.

What people don't understand is that mental toughness can be built, picked up, or learned. The main favorable position you have when you are brought into the world though is that you won't need to toil as hard to keep it or build up its level.

Getting mentally tougher resembles working out your muscles. If you lift loads constantly, at that point, you will get more grounded. The explanation that you get solid is on the grounds that your muscles react to the lifting of the loads. In a significant part of a similar way that you can work out your mind and make it tougher.

That is all well and good; however, how can one make it tougher, and to what extent will it take? Tragically, it can take some time, and it won't be the most effortless thing on the planet to do; however, it is totally conceivable. The ideal approach to make yourself mentally tougher is to step outside of your comfort zone as regularly as possible; by doing this, you are trying the cutoff points of what you want to and can't do.

A case of this would be in hand to hand fighting practice. Pushing yourself when you are drained, need to stop, or figure you can't handle it anymore are immaculate models. If you have practiced so hard that you figure you can't move a muscle and can't continue one increasingly minute, then pushing yourself to continue is the best approach to turn out to be all the more mentally tough.

Working through pain is another case of mental toughness. I need to note, however, that pain can mean that something is very wrong, and you ought to get it taken a gander at. There is a distinction between being hurt and being injured.

Being hurt is nothing genuine, and you can continue to work out. For instance, you may be hurt if your muscles are sore from lifting the prior day or If you have a headache. These, while irritating, won't cause any genuine damage and will assist you with building mental toughness. Being injured, then again, are things along the lines of breaking a bone, tearing muscles, or having a blackout. All are not kidding in nature and ought to be quickly looked at.

So remember that mental toughness can be built. It tends to be built by escaping your very own comfort zone and pushing, however, weakness, uncertainty, and pain.

Four Characteristics Essential For Mental Toughness

So with respect to mental toughness training. I don't require you to trust it's a type of training that you can build up through sets and redundancies. It's significantly more remote than that, and it requires some speculation, hard work, life encounters, and perseverance. You should see an association with your life and training to apply mental toughness training to your everyday life. Make sure to push yourselves, test your will, overcome torment, never give up, outwork people, learn to change pessimism into energy, overcome uncomfortable situations and fear, become strong in life and don't be a pushover, and carry that subdued beast that is at the gym over to this present reality, no doubt. Be MENTALLY TOUGH! Always remember, you are your most perceptibly terrible enemy! Concordance!

With respect to specific people, some are brought into the world mentally tough, and others are unquestionably not. Does this infer if you would one say one are of the people that aren't brought into the world mentally tough that you can never get tough? The fitting reaction is no.

What people don't comprehend is that mental toughness can be built, picked up, or learned. The primary ideal position you have when you are brought into the world though is that you won't have to work very hard to keep it or build up its level.

Getting mentally tougher takes after working out your muscles. If you lift stacks always, by then, you will get more grounded. The clarification that you get strong is because your muscles respond to the lifting of the heaps. In a critical part of a comparative way that you can work out your mind and make it tougher.

That is all well and good, anyway. How might one make it tougher, and to what degree will it take? Disastrously, it can take some time, and it won't be the easiest thing on earth to do anyway, it is absolutely possible. The best approach to make yourself mentally tougher is to step outside of your comfort zone as planned as could be expected under the circumstances; by doing this, you are attempting the cutoff purposes of what you need to and can't do.

A case of this would be in hand to hand battling practice. Pushing yourself when you are drained, need to stop, or figure you can't handle it anymore are impeccable models. If you have practiced so hard that you figure you can't move a muscle and can't continue one progressively minute, then pushing yourself to continue is the best approach to turn out to be even more mentally tough.

Working through pain is another case of mental toughness. I have to note, in any case, that pain can imply that something is wrong, and you should get it looked at. There is a qualification of being hurt and being injured.

Being hurt is nothing certifiable, and you can continue to work out. For example, you might be hurt if your muscles are sore from lifting the earlier day or having a headache. These, while disturbing, won't cause any authentic harm and will help you with building mental toughness. Being injured, on the other hand, are things along the lines of breaking a bone, tearing muscles, or having a power outage. All are completely serious in nature and should be immediately taken a gander at.

So remember that mental toughness can be built. It tends to be built by getting away from your own special comfort zone and pushing shortcoming, vulnerability, and pain anyway.

Chapter 8:
How to Develop self-discipline

Self-discipline can sometimes be defined or means living your life the hard way: opposing allurements and moment satisfaction, so as to get greater and better compensations in the future. It's surely simpler to maintain a strategic distance from a wide range of discomfort and entertain yourself at whatever point you need; however, at last, all that you get from that approach is transient joy now to the detriment of your future, which generally could have been vastly improved. Consider a feeble willed person who, when faced with a test, quickly quits. How likely is this person able to achieve anything significant in life if their essential worth is to feel comfortable? How is this person going to deal with an emergency that they should face? Indeed, even a moderately immaterial issue can turn into an unconquerable impediment for a person who's been living a shielded life and always maintained a strategic distance from what's difficult or unpalatable. Presently balance that with a person who willfully makes their life harder. They seek out and welcome difficulties as chances to grow. Every self-forced tribulation fortifies them, so fewer and fewer difficulties in life overpower them. Step by step, they inoculate themselves against issues correctly in light of the fact that they seek them out. At the point when life gives them an unexpected blow, they're ready to handle it on the grounds that — on account of living their lives the hard way — they're always ready for hardships.

It takes one minute to make the wrong choice and imperil your future. What feels like an unimportant decision today can have an extraordinary, enduring impact on your future. Every choice sets a point of reference — and when you make a similar wrong choice a few times in succession, it turns into your usual standard way of doing things. While one cheeseburger once in a while isn't probably going to demolish your general endeavors to get more fit, belittling the impact of more than once settling on the wrong choice can profoundly influence you through the span of the remainder of your life. Each time you are encountered with a decision between striving discipline and taking it easy, always tell yourself that the choice you're making today doesn't influence the present minute alone. A flashing decision can (and regularly will) resound for a long time or even a very long time into the future. People have the ability to act against their inclinations in exchange for a superior future. Lamentably, numerous people live by the rule of "If it feels good, do it, and If it doesn't, don't do it." Caving into your enticements at whatever point you feel them rise resembles giving up your humanity, as it were. As a clever individual, you have a capacity — and I daresay a commitment — to make decisions that depend on sound thinking, not on your impulses alone. Endeavor to be a superior human and grasp your humanity by practicing your "self-control muscle," rather than surrendering to your generally base (and least helpful for your long haul goals) part of the brain. Your most base senses may give brief comfort, yet only from time to time are good as long as possible, considering the exception of when there is an immediate danger to your survival.

A lot of people imagine that acting naturally disciplined means that you can sit before a flavorful bit of cake and gaze at it for a considerable length of time without eating it. They consider opposing allurements as resembling a knight defending his realm against the intruder. If you go to shabby bars each week, your likeliness of getting punched right in the face are greater than those of a person spending their nighttimes at home with a book. In like manner, the ideal approach to protect yourself against enticements is to maintain a strategic distance from them — and for that, plain old readiness is more significant than self-control. Your chances of undermining an eating regimen are higher If you have illegal nourishments at home. Expelling them from your home — a basic demonstration that requires little willpower, insofar as you're satisfied at the same time — will protect you when you get eager, and the desire to glut on them hits you like a huge amount of blocks. Your chances of staying in bed are lower If you set three unique cautions and place them away from your bed. You'll be less inclined to waste time at work when you hinder the most diverting sites as opposed to depending on your willpower to stop you before stacking those entertaining feline pictures. Set yourself up for difficult situations by setting up barricades ahead of time when your determination isn't being tried. Your self-control framework will do a portion of the truly difficult work for you, leaving your stores of self-discipline to be utilized for the impromptu situations when they emerge.

Self-discipline is a form of freedom. Freedom from sluggishness and dormancy, freedom from the expectations and requests of others, freedom from a shortcoming, and fear or uncertainty. Self-discipline enables a pitcher to feel his singularity, his internal quality, his ability. He is master of, as opposed to a captive to, his thoughts and emotions. Changing the manner in which you consider self-discipline can assist you with turning out to be progressively self-disciplined. All things considered regarding hardship and enduring, think about what! You might never find fun in personal growth, and in all probability, will before long give up on your endeavors. Then again, a person who considers self-discipline as a form of freedom will invite chances to practice their self-control.

When confronting allurements and contending energetically to not let them subjugate you, remember that through relinquishing them, you aren't losing anything generous; the freedom to be a master of your thoughts and emotions is at last worth more than any impermanent delight, of which you deny yourself.

Temperance isn't a mushroom, that springeth up of itself in one night when we are snoozing, or respect it not; however a sensitive plant, that grows gradually and tenderly, requiring a lot of pains to develop it, much care to protect it, much time to develop it, in our untoward soil, in this current world's harshly climate. If self-discipline resembled a mushroom that springs up of itself without the requirement for a gardener, everybody would have it. Sadly — or luckily, depending on what you look like at it — it's increasingly similar to a plant that you have to always develop, or else it wilts. A few people accept that one either has a "green thumb" or not — as though one person were brought into the world with an inherent ability to care for plants and another not. In all actuality, the person with the alleged green thumb is basically increasingly mindful of their plants. They make sure their plants possess everything they have to thrive and consistently determine their status to make sure they remain solid. Consider self-discipline similarly. You sow its seeds the instance you decide it's time to stop drifting through life and organize long haul awards over moment delight. In any case, this moment is only the earliest reference point; on account of planting the seed for another blooming plant, there's a lot of time and energy regardless you'll have to contribute to making it sprout. If you need to have a wonderful plant, you can't water it sporadically or move it beginning with one area then onto the next each other week. Solicit yourself: what sort of a gardener am I for my own self-discipline? If your self-control were a plant, how might it look dependent on how you've been developing it the past years?

THE VALUE OF SELF-DISCIPLINE

Self-discipline is by all accounts a "good old" idea, and not very numerous people talk about self-discipline nowadays.

If you need to be a top athlete, at that point, you have to spend years training, building up your skills, and showing signs of improvement constantly. It takes self-discipline to continue pushing yourself, to get up promptly in the mornings, to go to the gym when you feel tired, and to work through the pain.

If you need to be an entrepreneur, you will require the self-discipline to keep a positive frame of mind when people around you are losing confidence, to continue working for peanuts when the bills are mounting, to place in extended periods carrying out each responsibility that necessities, doing as opposed to taking a pleasant check to work for another person.

If you need to be a good salesperson, it takes self-discipline to hammer out those calls, to get out and meet potential customers, to accept the dismissal, to build new connections, and to build your "book of business."

If you need to be good at any career, it takes self-discipline to set up good work propensities, to push yourself to ceaselessly learn, to get outside your comfort zone, and to not be diverted from your objective.

The issue with self-discipline is that it is hard by its very nature; it means settling on choices that are focused on an end objective, as opposed to the "easy choices." Nearly anything that you can improve yourself or improve your life requires some self-discipline.

Chapter 9:
What Is Confidence?

The word confidence is seen as a term that is frequently hard to characterize. What is it, and what does it resemble? Are questions that can be inquired. Through the demonstration of correlation, one can see that there is a distinction between people with confidence and people that are not confident.

Instances of what confidence resembles are frequently taken from people in the entertainment industry. So: entertainers, performers, sports stars and moderators, and so forth.

The Meaning

The meaning, according to google.com, is - 1. The belief or feeling that one can depend on a person or thing; firm trust: "we had each confidence in the staff." 2. The condition of feeling sure about the reality of something.

This shows the general meaning of confidence is that one believes in oneself and in their ability to work and perform in life.

Society

Just as these roles that people play in the zone of entertainment, there are specific types of people that are viewed as the encapsulation of what confidence is in our society. Furthermore, this is generally depicted through the eyes of the mainstream media.

These are commonly the people that are portrayed as: good looking, skilled, fashionable, well off, and educated, for instance.

Childhood

Another surprising influence on the levels of trust we have is in the childhood years. The way they have been treated by carers and the way carers have treated others will also do an outstanding job in this regard.

Here one's caregivers can either make one feel confident in themselves or not. Furthermore, it might be that one was made to feel confident for what they did or what they had (outside) and not for what their identity was (Internal).

So their confidence was never disguised and incorporated; it was always based on some outside requirement being satisfied.

Outcomes

What at that point happens becomes the criteria of what confidence is and isn't. If one has what their childhood or society groups saw as confidence, at that point in principle, they will feel confident. What's more, based on those requirements, If one doesn't coordinate, they should feel unconfident.

The Exception

For each standard, there will always be special cases. People that are classed as alluring are sometimes confident, and sometimes they are definitely not. There are people who have mind-blowing ability and ability but then have no confidence in what they do.

Furthermore, being educated and having enormous aggregates of cash likewise doesn't ensure that one genuinely believes in themselves.

So does this imply If one has these, a couple of these, or even one of these requirements and still doesn't come near to being confident, that one has been sold a falsehood? Or then again, that one simply needs to continue gathering more?

Approval

After looking into it further of these cultural requirements and the requirements that were spread out in one's child, it turns out to be certain that these are altogether outside in nature. They are based on the acceptance and approval of someone else or people.

Furthermore, this means one is giving their power away to others. One is enabling someone else to characterize how one sees themselves and what one is fit off.

The Other Side

On the opposite side of people who don't feel confident, despite the fact that they have met certain requirements, are people who act confidently but then don't really coordinate to social orders beliefs of what it should have been confident. Or then again, they may have a couple of these requirements.

So how could these individuals be confident when they are not adhering to the guidelines of society or the requirements that were communicated in one's childhood?

Obviously, there will be a few people that have been empowered for who they were in their childhood and not adapted to the increased approval of others.

Permission

Since what these requirements are doing is giving one the permission to feel confident and to have confidence in what their identity is. These requirements, all by themselves, are impartial and are based on the conclusions and views of others.

So through accomplishing or having a specific requirement, the mind will have the option to satisfy certain expectations, which have come to fruition through the affiliations that have been connected to the requirement/s. What's more, this will, at that point, lead to the elusive experience known as confidence.

The benefit is that If one has these requirements, at that point, they can feel confident, yet this isn't always the case. It additionally means that one's confidence is at the impulse of others and outside conditions. Also, this will imply that one is being subjugated subsequently.

It resembles an undetectable web that all of us can turn into a part of, with no awareness. This web joins one emotionally and mentally dependent on others and places one’s sense of control into the hands of someone else or a gathering of people.

Models

One of the ways this way can be seen is the point at which one goes to another country or when an individual from another country comes to where one is. Here, one might have the option to see an unmistakable distinction in conduct, and this is on the grounds that their mind is deciphering the environment in an unexpected way.

What's more, this makes them behave in a way that could be viewed as freer or practically insubordinate when contrasted with one’s conduct or the conduct of others.

Interpretations

We are largely human, and we, as a whole, have an ego-mind. By utilizing the case of another country or a person who has resided in another country, it serves to accentuate the power of interpretation.

The manner in which we behave, how skilled we think we are, and to what extent our confidence is; is based on the interpretations in our mind. What's more, these are not fixed or unchangeable. They have happened through conditioning, and this can be changed.

The **Story**

So the statement 'Confidence doesn't exist' makes a lot of sense. In as much as, it is essentially a perspective. One may believe that they would lie or that they are misleading themselves if they somehow managed to consider themselves to be confident.

In any case, If one is assuming the role of not being confident, is there actually any more truth to this? It is just being seen as the truth due to it being a role that is being deciphered as natural and in this way sheltered to the ego-mind.

HOW TO BUILD CONFIDENCE

The initial step is a straightforward, however important one: purchase a medium estimated notebook. Use it for the composed activities in this program, likewise to record your encounters and screen your advancement. Date every section you make. Your notebook will turn into a good friend, instructor, and partner, so keep it close to you, counsel it consistently and update it routinely. Be committed to spending some time on this program each day. Only ten minutes every day – perusing, learning, thinking, doing, and so on – means more than 60 important long stretches of confidence-building movement a year from now. Twenty-five minutes a day builds as long as 152 hours in a year – that is close to 7 days! Would you be able to think about superior speculation for your future?

1. What difference would it bring to your life. If you knew undoubtedly that you could achieve anything.
2. Now consider three beliefs you would prefer to have, beliefs that would empower you and bring confidence.
3. Cross out the restricting beliefs and write these empowering beliefs in their place. What might you need to accomplish for these new beliefs to work out?

4. Make yourself entirely comfortable, either sitting or resting. Close your eyes and take a couple of full breaths and unwind. Enable your creative mind to stream freely. What might it be to be consummately confident? Let your mind float for a couple of moments; at that point, open your eyes and write down everything that rings a bell. Keep this rundown: you have it in your power to encounter this one day. Remember, whatever your mind can imagine and accept, you can achieve.

5. Commit yourself to act all the more confidently, as from now, regardless of whether it feels like a demonstration. Do what on-screen characters, artists, legislators, sports stars, and numerous others do the world over – pretend you're confident, regardless of whether you're most certainly not. For example, quiet your breath, stand upstanding, look at people without flinching and talk with an unmistakable, unfaltering tone: you will immediately feel progressively confident.

6. Beginning right now and into the foreseeable future, make this an unwavering principle: stop putting yourself down.

Never say anything regarding yourself, either quietly or so anyone can hear, that you don't earnestly need to be or work out as expected.

7. Decide right presently to treat yourself with adoration and regard and accept simply the best for yourself for the remainder of your life. Behind their open personae, many surely understood people, including the most charming and regarded, are urgently shy. In a radio station Terry O'Neill, the VIP picture taker whose photos of the rich and acclaimed have decorated reflective magazines everywhere throughout the world, depicted the Paramount Studios' century festivities in Hollywood. A hundred top famous actors were brought together, a significant number of whom needed to meet Elizabeth Taylor. O'Neill recognized her falling down in a corner, close to the entryway. 'I thought, nobody's going close to her,' he said as much, 'as I'd met her previously, I asked If I could help her. I brought up that every one of those people was here to meet her. She stated, "I'm so alarmed, Terry. I've never observed such a plethora number of stars in a single room." She was captivated – they all were! At that point, she asked me to acquaint her with Robert de Niro. I didn't have any acquaintance with him, yet I took her over, and it was stunning. It resembled seeing two bumbling children talking with one another.'

Importance of Self-Confidence

At the point when it's a matter of doing work In a particular state of mind, which will make that work better, at that point you've to make a friend about it and your ability. So prepare to go.

Self-confidence is one's ability to pass judgment on his own social and personal standing concerning his environment and have the option to infer satisfaction out of it.

Self-confidence is influenced by factors like childhood, work environment, and levels of commitment towards seeking after a reason. High confidence is a fundamental factor in improving business ties and adjusting to personal life.

There is a celebrated saying that when you start the voyage of your expert life, you believe in your abilities since you have not demonstrated your abilities yet.

Directly from the early times through the development of human society, this maxim couldn't be progressively exact with regards to the present. These are unfathomably focused times that we are living in, and self-confidence is one of the most critical pillars of solidarity and self-sustenance for an individual, more so now than any time in recent memory.

In this post, we will show you progressively self-confidence, and later you will learn increasingly about self-regard. So we should start this session by highlighting points to comprehend them better. We will show you the correct hypothesis and how to build your self-confidence as well.

How Confident are you?

What is confidence in any case, and how can it identify with self-esteem and self-image? Your self-image – the manner in which you see yourself – is made up of three center feelings and beliefs:

Self-worth: the worth you place on yourself – how comfortable you are and the extent to which you feel worthy of satisfaction and success.

Competence: your beliefs about your ability to achieve, take care of issues, and have an independent mind. This is the thing that I mean by confidence.

Having a place: regardless of whether you feel accepted and respected by others. Your appraisal of your self-worth and feelings of having a place make up your self-esteem. Your point is, obviously, to make confidence such a characteristic part of yourself that you seem confident on the outside as well as feel totally quiet with yourself inside. This is possibly achieved when each of the four components of the l-T-I-A Formula is joined. Intention and thought directly affect confidence, which is essentially a lot of beliefs about your gifts and capabilities. In any case, they have little impact on self-worth, which is principally emotional in nature, and as we as a whole know, intention, and thought have little influence over the emotions.

This is the place where creative minds and activity come in. Your inventive, creative mind directly affects the emotions and, giving they are sought after in the correct soul, so do your activities. Presently, to return to my unique inquiry, how's your self-worth? Do you accept you're competent to cope with life and achieve? Furthermore, do you feel accepted and respected by others? How confident would you say you are? If you purposely plan to be short of what you are equipped for, at that point, I caution you that you will be troubled for the remainder of your life. You'll be sidestepping your own capabilities, your own conceivable outcomes. Educator Abraham Maslow " How confident would you say you are? Rate yourself a mark out of ten, where ten tells that you feel you can achieve anything you desire (If you put forth a concentrated effort), and zero, that you feel absolutely unequipped for anything. (If you grant yourself ten, give this book to a friend – you clearly don't require it!) Now allocate yourself a mark for how high you might want your confidence to be. If you give yourself under ten, wonder why. Reflect on the grade you have given yourself.

" How high is your self-worth? Allocate yourself a mark out of ten, where ten means you feel worthy of all the good things life brings to the table, and zero, you feel totally worthless and undeserving. Presently give yourself a mark for how high you might want it to be. Once more, If you give yourself under ten, wonder why and reflect on the mark you have given yourself.

Do you feel that you are very much respected by others? Give yourself a mark out of ten for how well you relate to other people. Presently give yourself a mark for how well you might want to relate to other people. By and by, If you give yourself under ten, wonder why and reflect on the mark you have given yourself.

Take a huge bit of paper and draw a line down the center. At the top on the left, put down your first name or the name by which you are most popular (which could be an epithet). Underneath, depict how you feel about this name. Presently pick a name by which you might want to be known. Write it at the top of the right-hand segment. Who is this person? Fill this side of the page with notes about that person, who you envision them to be. At that point, look at the two segments. What does this let you know?

Grant yourself marks out of ten for how fulfilled you are with:

Your physical attributes: wellbeing, wellness, and appearance.

Your emotional make-up: would you say you are upbeat, a caring person, caring and considerate, quiet, and verify?

Your insight: your knowledge, skills, and capabilities.

Your social skills: how comfortable you become in social situations and what you accept others consider you. Reflect on why you have allocated these marks to yourself.

Write down what your potential is. What would you be able to attain if you had heaps of confidence? One thing is sure – you are fit for definitely more than you might suspect. A great many people's concept of their capabilities bears little connection to their genuine potential.

Smile at yourself using the mirror every morning; you'll be astonished what a difference it can make to your day. Even more, smile at yourself around evening time before resigning, as this brings sweet dreams and projects your intuitive mind to feel good about yourself. Confident people have no compelling reason to show off or force themselves on others. They may have high expectations of themselves; however, they likewise realize their self-worth is independent of their achievements and that they don't always need to be great.

HOW CONFIDENT ARE YOU? PLANT THE SEEDS OF CONFIDENCE AND SEE THEM GROW

Yesterday was just a dream, And tomorrow is just a vision. Be that as it may, today very much lived makes Every yesterday a dream of joy And each tomorrow a vision of hope Look well along these lines right up 'til the present time.

Show a portion of the factors in your life – including past events, people, and situations – which have influenced your confidence. How did they influence you? Presently, without making any decisions, consider how your frames of mind and beliefs, dreams, correspondence style, and activities have made your life. Write down anything that appears to be applicable.

Do you consider yourself dominatingly a thoughtful person or an outgoing person? In the end, do you enjoy your own company and easily get brought into your own inward world?

Or, on the other hand, do you get the greater part of your energy and motivation from the company of others? You can be confident in any case, and you unquestionably don't need to be noisy and gregarious. Being unobtrusively confident is similarly as fulfilling.

Commit yourself to take the important steps to turn out to be progressively confident. I realize numerous who enjoy examining the purposes behind their absence of confidence, however, fail to address it. Don't be one of them. Write these words on a clingy mark or little card and place it where you will see it first thing every day: 'I welcome each new day with a firm commitment to raising my confidence. I will carry out what is required to turn out to be progressively confident.' Whenever you see these words, smile and rehash them to yourself, with conviction, quietly or so anyone might hear, in any event, ten times.

Let's assume them as though you truly would not joke about this.

Consider one thing you might want to do that makes you nervous – nothing excessively requesting at this stage. Let yourself know again and again, 'I am enjoying (doing whatever it is). I realize I can do it, and I will.' Make yourself truly comfortable, either sitting or resting. Close your eyes and take a couple of full breaths and enable your creative mind to stream freely. Envision that you have heaps of confidence and are really doing whatever it is that makes you nervous. Following a couple of moments, open your eyes. Write down anything that rings a bell in your notebook.

Presently, if commonsense, feel free to do what you envisioned in Confidence Builder. Do not be put off by any uncomfortable feelings that emerge. You've recently put the I-T-I-A Formula into practice for the absolute first time.

Theory of Building Self-Confidence

Individuals need a kind of positive image about themselves, so they can identify their qualities and shortcomings. People with low confidence often pass into a mental state where everything turns into a shortcoming, and each perception seems personal. This prompts further self-debasement.

It is often seen that little children, particularly the individuals who have working parents, tend to divert their dejection as a fanciful friend. They talk to this "friend," solicit suppositions from him and by and large, are comfortable with the possibility of an imperceptible yet always present friend.

The greater part of them grow out of this stage in life when they start going to class and start making genuine friends; however, the voice always remains with them. Numerous people tend to give themselves either positive self-talk in the time of seeking motivation or negative self-talk in the time of handling failure and ensuing analysis.

Much the same as any preposterous person who is never going to budge on refuting you, the answer for handling and eventually quieting the "inward pundit" is likewise in having a quiet, legitimate, and goals arranged to talk with it. Attempt to enter a quiet exchange with it as that will assist you with identifying territories where your approach is not close to what others want out of you. It will allow you to acknowledge where you are going aimless with the goal that things can be brought back to follow.

There is nothing wrong with having a couple of defects. Given a need or want to change a couple of things about us, many would wish they could change or alter something or the other about themselves. In any case, that does not mean that we will continue nagging ourselves with a very basic view of things. For similar reasons, we should be compassionate in surveying others on their work and performance.

Remember that you can't fulfill everybody. It is simply impractical. There will always be scope for improvement, yet you have to think essentially with respect to what is the arrangement of parameters that you have to keep the quality of the output under.

Numerous characteristics go behind developing a strong personality. The first would be the ability to learn from failures and bounce back as fast as could be expected under the circumstances. Nonetheless, a forlorn person can't battle his way back to a usable express that early. It takes a lot of self-belief and coarseness to bounce back from a failure and recapture ground.

He would require a solid network of friends and partners who are supportive in nature and positive-minded in their approach. A strong person additionally has the quality to have the option to structure a practical arrangement and figure out how to execute it. Ridiculous targets and unthinkable requests are something that a person with flexibility would keep away from no matter what, just on account of the lesson he would have learned from his past failures.

Life is a hard instructor. It lets us bomb a test first and afterward, conveys the lesson of the lesson. While many may find it unjustifiable, that is the status quo. Presently, it is dependent upon whether you continue grumbling throughout each and every day about misfortune, botched chances, and the state of affairs turning out badly in life. Or on the other hand, you could decide that nothing more will be tolerated and it's about time that you got success in life.

We are surrounded by individuals who have faced in any event one major failure in their life. Though practically all surrender under the heaviness of that one major blame, there are rare sorts of people who utilized their failures as a springboard to move to more prominent statues.

It is found most times that passion can be temporary in nature. You may start on any endeavor with incredible intensity and fervor; however, it may so happen that following a couple of days, you will encounter the breeze getting knocked out of the notorious sail.

It is important to continue persuading yourself about your dream and where it is that you need to reach in the end. It is at precisely that point you will have the option to propel people around you to reconnect with full determination and included energy, much after they have faced destruction in the first round.

Modesty is an endearing quality to a lot of people. There's an idiom that enormity wonders you, commonality associates you. Modesty makes people love and regard you as they compare your success with your being unassuming. Nobody enjoys a person who's egotistical and unreasonably glad for his achievements.

Having said that, even modest people bomb on occasion. The difference is obstructing accepting a failure. Where forceful people will attempt to turn around and accuse anybody in their viewable pathway for a failure, an unassuming person would initially look inwards and identify territories of improvement in him before condemning anybody.

The manner in which you behave with people in the manner in which they remember you. Self-focused pompous people don't carry a persuasive quality around them. They were successful regardless of their unrivaled mentality, and not as a result of it. People would do well to comprehend the difference. Anyway, the times of these sorts of bossy people have since a long time ago come and gone, for good.

At the point when you are talking about creating solid connections, you are talking of quality, need, and adaptability. No relationship can get by on hostility and unlimited oversight lying with one person as it were. Welcoming and urging people to impart their insights with you makes them feel equivalent and important, which, in return, causes them to contribute better.

Passion is important to be a success in the face of affliction. The quality can motivate people to continue seeking after their goals, as passionate people don't like things they are not passionate about.

Senior enrollment specialists always give more importance to the measure of passion a youthful up-and-comer has towards his activity. The explanation being that If his passion goes past unimportant winning and nourishing the family, at that point, he will make one daydream of creating something new and bringing another activity for the company.

Chapter 10:
Why Need Confidence?

Being confident about your qualities encourages you to draw fortitude and goals when hard times arise in life. It allows you to keep things in context and back yourself when every other person says that the task ahead is about difficult to complete in the stipulated time.

A confident person has enough ability to comprehend his impediments and realizes how to make up for that with his determination and qualities.

Since we have seen how self-confidence depends on your apparent ability to deal with an action, we should examine the exercises that help to develop a sense of confidence.

Action That Helps Cultivating a Sense of Self-Confidence.

Self-confidence thrives in an air where the person is given productive feedback, and the main thing is always on the positive.

In such a working environment, a confident person will have the option to practice his skills and talent past expectations, as he will get an opportunity to set goals, overlook his own past mistakes, and learn new things.

Then again, a person's self-confidence can be seriously hampered in an environment where there is a steady examination with others and where expectations are unreasonable. People are set in opposition to one another according to their performance in the numbers game.

In these conditions, a person will be compelled to sustain an undesirable focused mentality by falling back on unjustifiable means for success, listening to unworthy role models, being excessively harsh in making a decision about his own performances, and thinking little of his own capabilities.

Such an environment breeds an undesirable workplace where the pressure is more on beating each other's performances, as opposed to meeting up as a team in aiding each other. Such organizations may top for quite a while; however, they eventually crash.

People with high self-confidence.

People with high self-confidence approach their issues diversely as compared to other people. They know the importance of building connections, and consequently, they love meeting new individuals to get and brainstorm new ideas. It is this quality of theirs that makes them amiable, as they are always ready to be in a discussion that gives equivalent importance and regard to each one of the individuals who have participated in it.

Confident people love communicating their ideas before others, as they are emotionally secure enough to take helpful reactions and reject emotional ones. That does not mean that they are presumptuous; despite what might be expected, they give everybody the opportunity to put their focuses forward. Be that as it may, they have the mental fortitude to adhere to their decision in spite of a lot of resistance to their ideas. If they are convinced what they are doing is correct.

There are two results to any decision taken – possibly it turns out to be the right one, or you come up short. In any case, what sets a confident person apart is that he doesn't need a manager around on depreciators when he succeeds.

In addition, a self-confident person has the quietude to recognize his mistakes and learn from them when he comes up short. This targeted approach towards both success and failure is the thing that makes a confident person an adorable and decent personality.

People with low self-confidence.

If compared to people with high self-confidence, people with low self-confidence have a harsh and basic view of themselves. They are inclined to make emotional decisions, as opposed to thinking judiciously. They tend to be in their "caverns" rather than meeting new people. They attempt to evade new companies and abstain from meeting new individuals.

An under-confident individual tends to feel that he has nothing significant or productive to add to any procedure. This feeling of low self-worth, joined with a complete disavowal towards any change makes an under-confident person very susceptive to abuse and undervaluation.

People with low confidence dither in imparting their thoughts and insights, as they figure their views will be disparaged in public. In addition to this, their past encounters and interactions with people have not done anything to improve their self-worth and change their views about their profitability and importance.

This is the place a beneficial climate comes into play. Each person learns from his environment, and your self-confidence depends legitimately on the sort of people you meet and the type of dialogs you have with them. While self-confident people collaborate with people whom they have something to learn from, under-confident people are convinced that they can't change and will be underestimated in spite of what they do.

Impacts of Low Self-Confidence

Each person needs somebody who he can adore and follow with the goal that he checks his own talents, achievements, and progress in contrast with that person and continually improves. This is actually what self-confident people do. While communicating with others, finding out about others, and putting their ideas in public to increase point of view, they always improve their skills and information.

Yet, what occurs when people stop doing that? They tend to lose sight of their focus, as they don't have any stay left in their life who can balance out them when they are getting loose. At the point when interacting with society is stopped, a person tends to consider himself, and that reflects in the manner he accepts analysis. Indeed, even productive analysis for his work will seem personal analysis for him, as his approach would have become incredibly self-focused at that point.

People with low self-confidence tend to conclude they have no talent or aptitude to complete a given task and be valued. In fact, certifiable acclaim for a good exertion comes to them an astonishment, and they see that as phony appreciation.

In conclusion, Self-confidence is just a generic term for many things. Emotional stress, humor, empathy, resistance, cordial relationships all help to create a personality that exudes confidence.

A confident person can say honest things without hurting others' feelings. A confident man also knows how to be heard with dignity when there are differences of opinion. Everything requires practice, but the most important thing is to believe that you can be better. It is the cornerstone of every improvement in the world.

Chapter 11: Compassion

Compassion is often one of the most important viewpoints a person can have. From helping us better understand our fellow individuals to assisting us with better understanding ourselves, compassion adds a sense of solidarity to our world, making our mutual voyages shorter and progressively blissful and instructing us that sometimes the best thing we can give somebody is the benefit of the uncertainty.

A fundamental part of life, certain laws, religions, and rules, particularly the "Brilliant Rule," all have a foundation of compassion. This is on the grounds that compassion, while being a virtue that fortifies the soul, additionally gives people the endowment of being better ready to identify with and relate to each other. This, eventually, gives us the keys to help one another.

Despite the fact that a simple enough idea, compassion isn't always that easy to pull from the breaks inside oneself, where it assuredly can be found. We often get excessively up to speed in the burdens and preliminaries of day to day living - the traffic, rushing, the long queues at the supermarket-to make compassion practiced workmanship. Be that as it may, through specific exercises, we can grow to have a superior understanding of what compassion genuinely is, the thing that it means to one's individual self, and how to completely grasp the blessings it imparts on our everyday lives.

Compassion was gotten from the Latin word, which in fact means "to endure with," yet compassion goes a long way past anguish. Joining sympathy, sympathy, care, and concern, compassion includes feeling for someone else and a readiness to express or share that virtue. Compassion includes looking past one's own life and plight and seeing at another, conditions, and soul. At the end of the day, compassion is caring put vigorously.

Compassion is real life can be as simple as rising up to let another person have your seat on the transport or allowing another car into your path in traffic. It very well may be donating holiday endowments to a nearby family out of luck, composing a hand-written letter or card to tell somebody that you're thinking of them, or talking to a friend about a battle that the person in question is having. Compassion can be in the form of a word, a hand, a look, a thought, or an idea.

Compassion is a concern for the welfare and prosperity of others. Compassion doesn't really require a focused love so as to exist; at the same time, it is often thought of as a form of love all by itself: a love for humankind overall. Compassion is contended to be the bedrock for generosity and selflessness, as compassion focuses attention outward as opposed to internal, and is a case of both sympathy (putting yourself from somebody's point of view) and sympathy (feeling miserable, sorry, or distressed on somebody's benefit, without essentially putting yourself in their situation).

Compassion is the reason for some strict ideas of love and is often referred to as a requirement for true philanthropy. All things considered, how might you develop the desire to help people a whole world away without feeling some measure of compassion toward them and needing to help in their plight?

Compassion is commonly viewed as the underlying foundations of non-profit organizations, social and mental work, and different substances intended to help other people, as these are made so as to help other people that are not straightforwardly known or engaged with their makers.

Compassion is not based on gender, no age, no nationality, no culture, no race, and no religion. It is a general worth. Likewise, compassion is indispensable to the worldwide estimations of love, harmony, uprightness, regard, and obligation, every single human worth that gives proof of caring, of seeing, of an ability to connect and make a difference, paying little heed to any apparent differences.

Further, compassion offers both short-and long haul benefits; logical examinations have shown that compassionate people produce even more a hormone that can slow down the maturing procedure and, to a lesser extent, a pressure hormone that can speed the procedure up. Likewise, compassion can engender more gratefulness, joy, and better connections. If you happen to be a parent or caregiver, a pioneer in your community, or just a concerned resident or friend, you can make yourself a paragon of compassion.

Following are five helpful tips for sharing and showing compassion in your community:

1. Make compassion a part of each and every day. At the point when you get up every morning, basically hold the word or the possibility of compassion in your mind for a couple of moments, deciding how you can offer somewhat more compassion during that particular day.
2. Focus on what you share for all intents and purposes with others, instead of your differences. Show your children to do likewise through exchange and demonstrating. Most enduring happens when we accept that we're isolated, as opposed to associated. Perceive that others are experiencing very similar

things you are - possibly not simultaneously or similarly, yet everybody wants to feel safe, happy, secure, and loved.

3. Practice irregular demonstrations of kindness. Pay for a stranger's espresso, leave a thoughtful, mysterious note for somebody who could utilize a lift, smile more, state "thank you" a lot. Little demonstrations of kindness and compassion can signify an entirely serious deal.
4. Practice cherishing kindness meditation. Put aside five minutes to find a comfortable, calm space, close your eyes, and sit up tall. Repeat the following expressions quietly to yourself: May I be safe? May I be healthy? May I be happy? May I live easily? (You can substitute different explanations that reverberate more with you If you like.) After three to five rounds, proceed onward to somebody you care about, envision that person in your mind's eye, and repeat similar articulations quietly to them: May you be safe. May you be healthy. May you be happy. May you live effortlessly. At that point, do something very similar, without judgment, for somebody who you battle with. In conclusion, send these thoughts of adoring kindness out on a worldwide level. Notice a warm glow from inside as you complete and sit quietly for a couple of seconds.
5. While compassion in real life is particularly powerful, don't be hesitant to talk about it and characterize it with your children. Tell them that compassion is important.

Chapter 12:
Love

Love is not diminished.

How would you characterize your love or your experience? How do you live at a comfortable level? I don't mean physically but emotionally and deeply. Some couples like the sentimental feelings of butterflies in their stomachs. They can talk about the feelings they feel as they think about their loved ones. Is love made to the mind, body, or both in all cases? Is love a thing or a shop? How would we know if we really loved each other? How simple is the total commitment to love? I do not consider myself a love expert or relationship mentor. I'm curious how it seems. What I do know is that love requires nothing from us because it is an empty vase to fill. It is simply a bond forever, where love is rarely recycled.

Is love unrestricted for you? Or otherwise, does it accompany requirements? What happens when those requirements are not met? Do you withhold your love for another? Is it conceivable to withhold the embodiment of what our identity is? How might we stop water flowing in a waterway? You may state: build a damn. Notwithstanding, if the dam isn't sufficient, the pressure of the water will find its way through or around it. You've no uncertainty seen tsunamis on TV where whole towns are overwhelmed by water. Water is a powerful analogy for love since it can improve a person's life, yet it can likewise be dangerous If it accompanies conditions.

Do we need love in our lives? What does love offer in return? Do you have a close or better understanding of others? Once, St. Francis of Assisi said, "It is by giving what we receive." He saw love as something that needed to be done to penetrate our lives and the lives of others. Love is like the sun, which gives its energy and does not require anything in return as it continues. The more love we give, the more we have. One wonders: what happens when love doesn't respond or when other people stop identifying with love? If love does not return, the ability of another to give or receive it does not diminish. The sun goes down every afternoon, and there are twelve hours of trouble. But with the cut of the first light, it reappears, carrying the energy to continue life. It is a cycle embedded in the texture of life, so it is with love.

Love extends wide and profound to incorporate the passionate issue you experience as your first love, the heart-beating love you feel when you see your child just because, and the delicate love you feel for your parents as they grow more seasoned. A consistent theme all through every one of these types of love is care and consideration for somebody. Eventually, that care and attention are best communicated through the word "compassion."

Dare To Fully Express Love

At the point when someone else stops cherishing us, it doesn't mean we are unlovable. For you can't stop the flow, it will normally find articulation in another form. Love is the counteractant to fear, disdain, and anger. It is the one true consistent thing in our lives that is offered to us from origination. We are naturally introduced to love and leave this life, realizing we will continue to love in the lifetimes that follow. The inquiry is: have you set out to completely express love in this life? Have you given love freely and unequivocally? We should resemble a wipe loaded up with water, completely wrung out when our time comes. We should fill our hearts with love and not withhold it for fear, or it won't be responded to. Since each time we take part in love, it is amplified inside each cell of our body. The more we give of ourselves, the more love grows inside our hearts. ,

Love is widely inclusive. All the healing in the world is introduced in Love, Divine Love. There are numerous strategies, yet one God. God is Love, Love is the wellspring of life, with Love you thrive, you have a reason to live. If love is pulled back, there is no reason to live, and the abhorrent continues. Malicious is life (spelled backward).

At the point when you have lived a life of struggle and fear, at that point, the devil is said to be in control. Devil is LIVED backward. This means as opposed to going ahead and advancing in life, and you are living life in backward movement, in the past hurts, emotions, events, and so forth. It is a struggle, and you are endeavoring and not flourishing.

A case of the impacts of lack of love is that of a woman who understands that her husband pulls back love from her. She becomes damaged by this to the extent of blaming herself or blaming it on black magic or shrewd spirits. She endeavors to win the friendship of her husband and goes to all lengths to verify his love. She may feel that life is a struggle and isn't worth living or even endanger her life by engaging in edgy acts like battling, counseling prophets, entertainers, and so on to get love parts to regulate her husband.

1. SELF LOVE

Love along these lines is key so as to thrive as an individual, not to mention a woman. At the point when you focus inside yourself and start tending to your personal issues, it could associate with confidence, fears of dismissal, or low self-esteem; at that point, you have started a procedure of healing of SELF, and this is simply the beginning of Love. The outcomes are supernatural in that your inward work begins to show ostensibly when you gain more confidence, begin to grow and bloom and gain in self-esteem. A woman who experiences this internal work is a magnet to people around her as she begins to pull in healthy connections, discard unhealthy, skewed connections. She gets appealing and enjoyable to be near and may end up verifying the love that she is frantically seeking.

2. LOVE ANOTHER

For you to love someone else, you have to love yourself first. Disdaining yourself or putting yourself last really opens you up to maltreatment. A woman who is always scrutinizing herself and contrasting all her highlights with others will accomplish more damage to herself as well as other people. She will lose self-regard and do deplorable things. A woman of free ethics is one who doesn't love herself enough to have esteemed in life. Despite the fact that she may guarantee that conditions compel her, in established truth, it is a lack of self-love and self-control. Since she despises herself so much, she focuses on gaining something at all expense. You can possibly love someone else. If you love yourself first despite the conditions. This is genuine love.

3. LOVE YOUR CREATOR

Many people understand this divine mandate but do not know that it depends on the previous two. How can you love your creator if you can't love his creation? If you believe you love God but hate yourself or someone else, you should reconsider your statement. The complete command is to complete the love of your creator by loving yourself and loving the other as yourself. Only when reconciled, can life begin to flow easily.

Chapter 13:
Love and Compassion

Regardless of whatever your identity is or where you originate from, without compassion and love for yourself and the environment around you, you will never get the opportunity to enjoy success for what it is. Despite the fact that humans generally have various preferences, there is common among all of us that common is the requirement for giving and getting compassion and love.

A wide range of success starts with your thought procedure, and If you did exclude love and compassion in that procedure, you would always feel like there is something missing in your life. That insatiable person I depicted before would relate to that in his moments of profound thought without anyone else's input. The thing is, we form propensities simpler than we accept, even those of us who appear to be so solid.

Love and Compassion

The holy energy of love and compassion, the Great Heart of the World, grasps every one of us, without condition, bringing together the entirety of life, joining the entire creation inside the warm soul of kindness, thankfulness, and concern. With favorable luck, we may meet people in whom this liberated love sparkles firmly, allowing all-around to relax in its light. The extraordinary holy people and bodhisattvas, totally purged of themselves, transmit such love and compassion. In certain occurrences of collective love, the substance of this unfathomable sea of love may encompass the entire get together. It might enter a substantial marriage and may inform the bonds among parents and children. At whatever point we investigate someone else's eyes and recognize the equivalence, that that person and I are the equivalents, not separate, this is love.

Despite appearances in actuality, Divine love and compassion suffuse each edge of the world, even our own. Divine love remains before the formidable inconsistencies in our lives: our God-given freedom that offers the guarantee of profound bliss just as the suffering attendant on living. The Divine heart of compassion praises the beauty of the freedom inside every person, and a festival made ambivalent by the cost of freedom: inescapable suffering.

At the point when we know about or see someone else's adversity, and we feel the ache of their suffering and are moved to extend the assistance that exists in our power, this is compassion. For this, we need strength since suffering falsehoods surrounding us. The everyday news' reiteration of disasters and fiendishness deeds, enormous and little, could annihilate us, where we got up to its entirety and lacked the strength to hold up under it. However, arousing, through profound practice, brings its preferred position. What's more, the suffering we see is more than adjusted by the delight that flows to us alongside love, protecting the compassionate from being overpowered by the power of pain.

Widespread lovelies a long ways past its pale impersonation in the lower energies, where emotional connection turns from "love" to despise, jealousy, or despondency. By and by, the world is developed to such an extent that it stays inside our conceivable outcomes to participate in love intentionally. However, that can just happen to the degree we void ourselves of ourselves.

Self-referential thought processes, self-centeredness, connection, desire for something in return, getting a handle on, a set of conditions, partial-heartedness - none of these have wherever in love and, in practice, completely hinder the action of love. Putting ourselves first and at the middle forecloses the plausibility of love. However, moments do come even to us, maybe with our family or our pets or unexpectedly with a stranger, when we are quickly free of egocentric connection, and the true heart of target love opens inside us. In unguarded moments, our common reaction to people is friendship, one of the faces of love. To have the option to love is an objective elevated and worthy enough to support our long adventure along the way, drawing us ever forward.

Our common mother, the Earth, likewise loves, loves every single one of us and all life in her biosphere. Like a self-focused and touchy child, we just also once in a while return this love. Furthermore, similar to a child, we so underestimate the love of our mom Earth that we don't recognize it. However, her love is there for us independently, in nature and in the city, If we can yet open to it. One simple articulation of it shows the beauty with which nature embellishes herself. Also, there are other more straightforward articulations we may see, including a store of otherworldly energies inside the Earth that we can draw upon. In any case, as a species, we have to develop and not anticipate that the Earth should continue uncertainly engrossing each affront and damage we heap upon her. We push these cutoff points at the Earth's and our risk. The Earth gives and gives and gives, maybe beyond what she can manage. But since our aggregate strength currently surpasses our aggregate insight, the Earth needs us to find a place in our hearts for her. By our internal work, by opening to higher energies, by decontaminating our will and intentions, we help wash down our group will, raise our aggregate degree of being, and give back to the Earth and human society. What's more, we do this for love.

Love manifests in many ways, but it always reveals our inherent unity. The unmistakable seal of love dissolves our veils of isolation and separation, allowing us to be complete on our own in the sweet aroma of fusion. Because of love, we are born, and in love, we leave. In the middle, we seek to love and find love.

The world of universal love, a world beyond all forms, even beyond the realm of light, corresponds to the planets known as Atzilut (emanation) in Kabbalah and Lahut (Unlimited) in Sufi cosmology.

How To Express Compassion And Love

It truly is very simple to express these emotions genuinely to others. The principal thing you have to do is dispose of the "what would I be able to escape their attitude." Indeed you realize the one we have all attempted it sooner or later in life, and perhaps you're yet attempting to arrive at your very own success with that attitude.

Treating others with compassion and love is just conceivable when you trust you are notable for giving it, not whether they deserve it or not. It sure is easy to think of numerous reasons why others don't deserve it. What about thinking of reasons why they do?

Feeling helpless is something people fear incredibly, and it appears we have put compassion and love into that category without understanding its outcomes. To show love and compassion towards others possibly makes you powerless when you can't utilize the word no when you have to. I sure have learned that one.

What Does Success Resemble When Compassion And Love Are A Priority?

It doesn't have an enormous ego that is, without a doubt, better still, and it doesn't utilize and mishandle others for monetary profit. It is the point at which you are so comfortable with helping others you don't consider it, and you do what needs to be done normally. Ask any successful person, and they will reveal to you that having compassion and love and helping others is the manner by which they got to where they are.

At the point when compassion and love are applied to one's life while attempting to achieve success, it emanates through your body language and outward appearances. This is because of the contentment felt by treating yourself as well as other people precisely as you ought to and having the option to apologize when you haven't.

Chapter 14: How to Develop the Power of Love and Compassion

Love and compassion join families, friends, and networks together consistently. The strength of your connections depends on how much love and compassion you have in your mind. The more love and kindness you have, the more you enjoy your connections with others, the more you feel appreciation, thankfulness, and happiness. Without love and compassion, it's absolutely impossible you can connect personally with others. Developing compassion and love is the most important thing you can do in your life.

- What is love? Love genuinely wants others to have happiness and have causes and conditions for happiness.
- What is compassion? Compassion honestly wants others to be free from suffering and the causes and conditions of pain.

Some people have denied connections and connections. They do not immediately understand why they cannot communicate well with others. The development of love and compassion will contain this conundrum. At the point when you have love and compassion, you see your connections thrive normally, and each interaction you have as comfortable and fulfilling.

Without love and compassion, connections can feel self-cognizant, unfilled, and pulled back. Be that as it may, when you develop love and compassion, your connections become healthy, characteristic, straight-forward, and comfortable.

Everybody has love and compassion somewhat. However, we, as a whole, need to grow, strengthen, and develop that quality. If you meditate on love and compassion steadily, you will improve an increasingly rich experience. As you do this, after some time, all aspects of your life turns out to be all the more warm and distinctive.

How would we meditate on compassion and love?

Strengthening your compassion and love isn't something that occurs incidentally. In the first instance, you have to have positive thoughts and emotions to create the correct environment. Without a positive mindset, you won't have the option to connect with others or even be happy. Those positive thoughts and emotions are liable for happiness, satisfaction, and contentment.

You can't focus on love or compassion for only a solitary day to create it. However, you have to shift your focus after some time toward positive thoughts persistently. You have to recognize and think about what love is and what compassion is.

At that point, regardless of whether you are sitting quietly or associating with others, regardless of where you are or what you might be doing – at work, at home, at a café, and so on., focus your mental attention on others and think "They are much the same as me. As I don't have any desire to suffer, they additionally don't have any desire to suffer." Do this as often as possible.

As you train your focus along these lines, at that point, after some time, you start to experience love and compassion, and the mindset emerges in you that you wish for others to be happy and not to suffer.

The more you focus along these lines, the more grounded your positive energy develops.

The reason we possess anger and other negative feelings is that we focus our attention such a great amount on the reasons for those feelings. Rather, the more we focus our attention on love, the more it turns into a more grounded tendency in our minds. Compassion is comparable: when we focus on needing others to be free from suffering, we develop sympathy. We create the attitude that we don't need others to experience suffering or the reasons for pain.

When you experience the positive feelings of love and compassion through this meditation, after some time, your attitude toward everybody will shift. You start sending positive energy from you to the world, creating more happiness and amicability. What's more, as your attitude shifts, the world will send back that sort of positive energy to you, which will have an astounding benefit in your life.

That is the power of compassion and love.

How Does Love And Compassion Sustain Humanity?

Love and compassion are certainly the characters of human life. We can't envision humanity without them. Indeed, even creatures, who have less thinking capability than us, display their tendency to love and care for their race. The manner in which a mother monkey carries her dead newborn child much after its demise is nothing yet an indication of love and connection.

Very same is with humans. Indeed, even before beginning our human life, love and compassion came in. At the point when a baby is in the belly of their mother, he is completely at her love and care. From the air that he inhales to the sustenance that he receives is received from the mother. At that point, after he is conceived, a baby is completely dependent on his mother. A baby isn't able to do its own. Thus it is the love and care of his mother that makes him live.

So being a mother itself is the best case of love and compassion. The measure of penance a mother needs to do to bring up a child is huge and can't be compared to anything in the world. A few people would differ, saying it's the obligation of a parent to do as such, and thus there is nothing uncommon about what parents accomplish for a child. However, at that point, they ought not to disregard the cases we hear when infants are found lying in the dustbins and to the leniency of the Lord.

Why are Love and Compassion so Important?

The world, If we look from a human life point of view, is brimming with catastrophes, problems, pains, and sufferings. The greater part of the people is encompassed by problems that afflict their happiness. So someplace we as a whole suffer. The reason and size can contrast. Yet, If we just care about our problems and sufferings, at that point, humanity itself will be addressed. Here comes the requirement for compassion. At the point when we attempt to understand the pain of others and how they are feeling in a painful situation, at that point, we attempt to support them. If not more, we, at any rate, don't attempt to increase their problems.

Sympathy and compassion are needs of great importance. People befuddle these perspectives with sympathy. People in pain needn't bother with sympathy, yet they need to be felt for. Attempting to feel what others are experiencing and afterward helping them in any way conceivable is what is required. It is hence that love and compassion are not an extravagance but rather a need.

When are Love and Compassion Needed?

There is no particular point in time when we need love and compassion. Or maybe they are a part of our essential nature. The fundamental part of being a human being is to be sympathetic, adoring, and compassionate at the point when we see a person who is in a tough situation, we should attempt to put ourselves in his perspective and afterward attempt to feel what the person should be going through. This procedure makes us aware of what our optimal conduct ought to resemble.

For instance, If we see a physically crippled person, at that point, we should attempt to be compassionate towards them. Here we are not instructing you to show them sympathy. This is the least that is required. Or maybe we ought to understand the sufferings they are experiencing and attempt to diminish their pain by being truly sympathetic and treating them ordinarily and not doing things that would dishearten them.

Further, If we see a pregnant woman on transport or train, we should offer her a seat. It isn't only a part of valor for men but, on the other hand, is material to women. If a woman won't be compassionate for other women, how might we anticipate that men should be sympathetic for women since they are physically extraordinary and hence understanding the pain and hardships of pregnancy is progressively difficult?

Love and Compassion are Necessities

We should consistently attempt to feel what someone else is experiencing. This will assist us in understanding their condition and will empower us to be thoughtful. There are occurrences when people mock somebody's diseases. This is nothing yet the lack of compassion in them. Doing this increases the hardships of the person already in pain.

Love and compassion are a perspective that ought to be with every one of us the time. We shouldn't be a holy person to practice this in life. There are endless moments when we can shower love and care for others.

The feelings of compassion and love are not confined to different humans yet additionally apply to animals and other living creatures. Since we are the most developed of the considerable number of animals on the planet, it is an additional duty regarding us to be considerate to animals and other lower species. It is just these feelings that make us unique or more than some other living being on the planet.

Why is having an enormous heart important?

Have you at any point heard someone state to another that another has a little or cold heart and mean it as anything besides an affront? In any event, when backed by facts, it's anything but a compliment, isn't that so? Presently consider the inverse, have you at any point heard somebody state that another had a huge heart, and not mean it as a compliment?

Love is at the focal point of having a huge or warm heart. If you can feel any of the kinds of love, from sentimental right down to fondness or brotherhood, you're nearly there.

By adding compassion to a base of love, you have a foundation for an incredible life. Compassion for other people and for yourself means you can put yourself from their point of view and understand how they feel. It doesn't imply that you need to accept their qualities or endorse their actions.

This comprehension and the love of our fellow humans can assist in investing up our differences. There will always be rubbing between people. Having the devices to help make things go all the more easily and to forgive others their minor offenses. How would you figure things would go If we as a whole had cold and little hearts?

In what aspect can I apply this in my life?

Think about the point in your life when you tend to be least adoring and least compassionate. Again, remember that being compassionate doesn't require to agree with or condone the beliefs or behaviors of an individual or group of people.

Are there particular groups of people or times or conditions which cause you to harden your heart? Why would that be? What about your rules or expectations have they neglected to cling to or broken? Again, you don't need to agree with them or their behavior to have a warm heart.

The initial phase, in my mind, is to understand yourself. When you understand why you are having an issue with a person or group of people, or behavior that is common to them, you have a likelihood to understand yourself. By understanding yourself, you can better and all the more easily understand them.

Shouldn't something be said about these events that cause you to harden your heart towards them? While their actions might be loathsome, they are still individuals from the human race. If you can block them for that behavior, to what extent before you cut out people with less extreme behavior? When do you halt moving the line?

What percent of the individual on the planet matches your guidelines, and how would you treat the individuals who don't? Is this progressively a proportion of what their identity is or of what your identity is? If you accept that the former (they are), at that point, there is minimal more in this post for you. I just ask that you set aside some effort to consider what has been talked about in the sections above.

For the individuals who believe that such an attitude says more regarding you than about them, I would state that I agree. What's more, the attitude I hold in my heart says more regarding me than it says about any other individual, as I am the one in particular who has any power over my heart, and whether it is warm or cold.

Until we apprehend the reason we harden our hearts, we won't have the option to change our attitude, isn't that so? Try to figure out what specific beliefs or rules they are violating. If you simply state "it's wrong," you won't have a lot to work with, isn't that so?

The last thought is to consider the rules or beliefs which they are violating and consider how their rules and beliefs are extraordinary. While your rules and qualities are clearly better than theirs, what would you be able to do to allow them some tolerance in their behavior?

The world is turning into a little place, and we will continue to communicate with more people from different parts of the world. Having a warm heart, coupled with the ability to show love and compassion, will turn out to be increasingly more important as time passes.

9 798201 104245

www.ingramcontent.com/pod-product-compliance
Ingram Content Group UK Ltd.
Pitfield, Milton Keynes, MK11 3LW, UK
UKHW020124290926
15471UKWH00003B/263

9 798201 104245